Jarema Drozdowicz

The Symbolic Dimension

ETHNOLOGIE

ANTHROPOLOGY

Band / Volume 58

LIT

Jarema Drozdowicz

The Symbolic Dimension

Anthropological Studies in Culture, Religion and Education

LIT

This book is printed on acid-free paper.

Bibliographic information published by the Deutsche Nationalbibliothek
The Deutsche Nationalbibliothek lists this publication in the Deutsche Nationalbibliografie; detailed bibliographic data are available in the Internet at http://dnb.d-nb.de.

ISBN 978-3-643-90539-0

A catalogue record for this book is available from the British Library

Klosbachstr. 107
CH-8032 Zürich
Tel. +41 (0) 44-251 75 05
Fax +41 (0) 44-251 75 06
E-Mail: zuerich@lit-verlag.ch
http://www.lit-verlag.ch

LIT VERLAG Dr. W. Hopf
Berlin 2014
Fresnostr. 2
D-48159 Münster
Tel. +49 (0) 2 51-62 03 20
Fax +49 (0) 2 51-23 19 72
E-Mail: lit@lit-verlag.de
http://www.lit-verlag.de

Distribution:

In the UK: Global Book Marketing, e-mail: mo@centralbooks.com
In North America: International Specialized Book Services, e-mail: orders@isbs.com
In Germany: LIT Verlag Fresnostr. 2, D-48159 Münster
Tel. +49 (0) 2 51-620 32 22, Fax +49 (0) 2 51-922 60 99, E-mail: vertrieb@lit-verlag.de

In Austria: Medienlogistik Pichler-ÖBZ, e-mail: mlo@medien-logistik.at
e-books are available at www.litwebshop.de

Contents

Introduction

By participating in culture today, we are submerged in an immensity of strands, artifacts and factors, the historic provenance of which becomes increasingly vague – and sometimes it is also even completely irrelevant from the point of view of people who incorporate these elements into their particularistic identities. The world has currently become diverse in terms of articulating cultural needs. Moreover, it is now ready to satisfy these needs much more willingly than it was in the past, when dissimilarity with regard to the predominant pattern has been treated unvaryingly in terms of social deviance or exoticism until recently. However, the diversity of today's global culture is embedded in a certain context of development, i.e. the historic process of forming today's beliefs, attitudes and motivations for social action. Seen from this perspective, culture becomes a territory where given individuals and groups are active and where they pursue some peculiar "cultural guerrilla warfare" with the help of various strategies that allow them to mark and show their existence in a manner of both a present and future valorization of otherness as such. Today the difference formula seems to be crucial when it comes to the understanding of contemporary cultural phenomena. It comes as no surprise to anyone today to observe the extreme individualization of attitudes, the counter cultural withdrawal from the ruling system of social norms, the doctrine of shock within the sphere of aesthetics, or the legitimization of mere kitsch within the sphere of high culture.

We have grown accustomed to the multicoloured reality, even if it means moving away from a certain resource of tradition and heritage. On the other hand, we also speak of the world being much more homogeneous today than it used to be in the past. It has become more monochromatic in its shades of lifestyle in the wake of globalization and the triumphant march of consumerist culture. Notwithstanding this, we are also willing to reconcile ourselves to the global world order, provided that we receive satisfactory gratification in the form of a provisionally understood resource of acceptable forms of identity that the media, popular culture, or everyday practice provide us with. Thus, the new reality order seems to define our understanding of culture anew and in many cases it also seems to invalidate what does not befit the new way of life, i.e. local character, traditions, territory, or the sphere of our beliefs. All these spheres of human agency seem to sink into oblivion, along with the cultural change that favours what is up-to-date, technologically perfect and fashionable. Therefore, it remains open to debate whether there is room for phenomena, actions and forms that do not inscribe themselves into the scheme of globalization in a world which has been so perfectly structured in terms of technology.

Of course, the image of the transformations of contemporary times, outlined above and considerably simplified, is only an attempt to signal certain trends and processes representative of the current cultural condition of the world. Notwithstanding these, many phenomena, which are up-to-date by all means, seem to reject the argument of the profound influence exerted by globalization and the homogenization of culture. Apparently, culture is a human quality which breaks free from any attempts to schematize it and to make an instrumental use of it within the scope of specific discourses. These discourses also include the scientific conception and all which involves the research of culture. Today culture becomes the subject of the interest of humanities in spheres which used to be overlooked and treated as not meeting the requirements of scientific authority until recently and, what follows, as impossible to be described in an objective manner. At present, however, we notice a significant increase in the interest expressed by researchers who represent various branches within the scope of the humanities and social sciences, where they concentrate their research efforts on the attempts of understanding the dynamics and the substance of cultural change taking place right before our eyes. Of course, contemporary cultural studies also raise topics which belong to the problem of the cultural consequences of globalization outlined above. Nevertheless, in many cases these problems are treated as a certain starting point for a much more profound reflection on the place of culture in human life and the analyses of contemporary cultural phenomena conducted owing to this research, and show the conceptual ambiguity of many, seemingly already well-recognized, transformations of reality. However, the blurring of the subject of research in cultural studies results not only from the very liquid character of postmodern reality. The area of the theoretical and methodological rationale behind many branches of humanities and social sciences pursued today is another source of research disputes. The branch in which internal disputes and the impedimenta of academic tradition form a particularly noticeable factor that directly influences the concepts of culture defined by it, is cultural anthropology.

The optics of today's anthropological research is a highly complex set of research proposals, methodological stances and a specifically anthropological approach to cultural phenomena. Culture, in both its general dimension as a pan-human quality and expressed in its particular manifestations of local cultures, is put in the centre of anthropological considerations. It is this unique character that contributed to the emergence of anthropological thought from the social sciences at one time, along with a simultaneous crystallization of the subject of research in anthropology at the turn of the 19th and 20th-century. At present, however, the theory, method and subject of anthropological studies seem to blur in the context of a decline of the traditional field of study for this branch – the exotic and spatially distant "savage" who represents cultures and communities, the customs and beliefs of which are equally distant from the Western patterns as their archaic world view is. Therefore, a countless host of scholars set off in order to search the most hidden areas of the globe for those last tribes who have not had any contacts with us, or they kept reading equally exotic otherness into the folk culture of the rural regions of Europe. For a long time, anthropology used to appropriate the formula of cultural difference, offering its time and resources to maintain the *status quo*. The problem is, however, that inasmuch as such actions were legitimate within the field of social sciences in the days of Bronisław Malinowski or Franz Boas, today the same field of study has become somewhat of a trap for anthropology. It has been forced to undergo an internal transformation as a result of the transformations of reality surrounding us all, as well as due to the processes of change that take place within the sphere of social theory.

The concept of culture began to be widened and defined anew, along with the emergence of increasingly numerous doubts as to the legitimacy of ruling theories. One of such significant turns of events was the set of changes which had been visible in anthropology towards the end of the 1960s, when the fatigue of the structural method started to be clearly sensed. Both cultural anthropology and the sciences akin to it witnessed the process of giving rise to certain lines of enquiry, the common denominator of which was the meaning of cultural phenomena in the semantic sense. Interpretation of meanings and symbols of culture started to be perceived as a chance of obtaining a fuller description of reality provided by anthropological fieldwork. The trend of symbolic anthropology, which developed in the Anglo-Saxon context in the 1970s, inscribed itself well in the transformations mentioned above, at the same time being an anthropological spin-off of a much wider theoretical movement known as the cultural turn (or the turn in interpretation). Since then, the ways which cultural anthropology has taken became marked with interpretative postulates and the textual metaphor, as well as with the interest in the problem of key meanings for a given culture. These selected research problems also find their distinct overtone today and the symbolic current has not lost much of its initial punch and freshness. Although speaking of the symbolic side of culture today is burdened with many objections (e.g. political ones), the turn in thinking of what culture is as such, and how particular local cultures or cultural phenomena of contemporary times situate themselves in it, cannot be reversed. Today, we think of the semantic level of culture in the first place, studying religious rituals celebrated on the island of Bali and Western subcultures embedded in pop culture with equal attention (preserving, of course, the unique character of a given context) and treating these phenomena as disparate manifestations of a common level of ideas which manifest themselves through human activity and material creation.

To a large extent, this collection of articles is an attempt to take a closer look on the symbolic perspective with regard to the problems that emerge in the sphere of the cultural transformations of contemporary times, educational processes and institutions, as well as the sphere of beliefs and the forms of religious life. In my opinion, these three subject areas constitute an important factor in the shaping of human identity. It is so because the aspect of identity occupies a central position in today's cultural discourses that emphasizes the diversity of contemporary forms of auto-identification, as well as their unique character resulting from the process of cultural change. The context of this change has also been marked with the influence of globalization processes, which are defined here not only as a global movement of content, models and artefacts, or a global network of economic, political or cultural connections, but also as a new type of global self-awareness of both individuals and groups. It is a kind of a global world view, in which identity is being structured through connecting together even some elements of dissimilar cultural provenance without causing any detriment to the consistency of the structure of that very identity. Examples of such seemingly self-contradictory structures can be found everywhere today. Regardless, however, of whether we speak here of the new American subcultures, national debates on multiculturalism, the conceptualization of unfamiliarity or some new religious movements, the contemporary activities that aim at a valorization and legitimization of identity, gain widespread acceptance.

The anthropological thought was one of the elements that has largely contributed to this state of affairs. From the very beginning of their autonomous existence, anthropological studies on cultural diversity defined the concept of difference as a given reality. It is so because ascertainments of this kind were confirmed by field data and the remarks resulting from it. In this regard, the ethnographic narratives created at the beginning of the 20th-century were connected to one another not only by a fascination with cultural otherness, but also by the need for penetrating and explaining the intricacies of puzzling rituals, symbols, or practices. In the classic anthropological approach, human behaviour, thoughts and material creations are naturally diverse to some extent, much like the biological aspect of human beings-in-the-world is. Although today the racial discourse in anthropology contends with the historical burden of racism understood in terms of ideology, politics and social practice, the issue of building the category of difference based on biological conditions seems now to return in the humanist discourse. This topic is reflected particularly in educational issues, where the character of the educational process, the way in which schools and universities operate, the educational policy or particular educational programs still remain infiltrated (particularly in the Unites States) by a number of prejudices, more or less implicit stereotypical representations, as well as the mechanisms of selection and stratification based on ethnic and racial affiliation.

In this context, the texts published in this volume refer not only to the tradition of the symbolic current, but also to the formula of the anthropology of education. This trend, the popularity of which we can trace from the 1950s until now, chooses the processes and phenomena of an educational nature, understood as an emanation of a specific cultural order in both social and institutional space, as its goal. The fact that this current exists at the meeting point between two branches – cultural anthropology and pedagogy – is significant. The interdisciplinary character of the anthropology of education makes it possible to put particular cultural phenomena into a wide perspective of culture transmission processes and other processes related to it, e.g. cultural assimilation or the immigrants' adaptation. A scientific description generated owing to such a measure contains theoretical and methodological elements of both anthropology and pedagogy, whereby they are treated in a complementary manner. It gives rise to the possibility of adopting a holistic view on changes that take place within the scope of global cultural ecumene at present, as well as with regard to particular examples of change taking place at the local level. The formula of the anthropology of education provides us with the possibilities of examining the problems mentioned above through putting them into a given context. The context encompassing the phenomena described above is marked in terms of meaning, and it is precisely the changes taking place at the level of meanings and cultural symbols that constitute the main subject of considerations presented in this volume.

Part I

Symbols and meanings in anthropological theory and education

Chapter 1

Interpretation of culture from the perspective of symbolic anthropology

Every time one defines the limits of any trend in science, regardless of whether the point is time limits or ideological affiliations, it seems a bit like a breakneck task. It requires particular self-discipline, considering that making an exclusionary selection from among all the possible intellectual influences, historical contexts and the impact of a number of other factors, can be easily questioned. It is because there is always the danger of overlooking some problems that are significant from a specific point of view and constitute the theoretical and methodological genesis of such a trend. Such an approach to the problem may also impel one to adopt a simplified evolutionary and genetic view on the shaping of particular specialties within a given branch. I would regard this approach, however, as erroneous and as the one that clouds the picture of the issue. It is especially so because of the very particularity of anthropology; indeed regardless of whether the point is cultural or social anthropology, ethnology or ethnography, it requires the adoption of an open attitude – a broad view on all possible surprises, from both the examined objects and the subjective impression that controls the researcher.

Doubt is being cast today on the thesis that science develops in a linear manner through inevitably developing an accumulation of knowledge and subsequent revolutionary watersheds – this is a thesis which has been perceived as a paradigm until recently. The grounds for this view, undermined from different sides in recent decades, have been shaken mainly due to the increasing interest in perspectives that fit among the terms that are far-famed today: "relativism," "deconstructionism," "textualism," and especially the widely understood slogan of "postmodern philosophy." Although these thought currents are being fiercely fought down by representatives of some scientific circles and the departed luminaries of postmodernism are slowly transforming their theses, some value should be conferred to them, at least for one reason. Through undermining our foregoing dogmatic convictions and grafting suspicion towards "long-range" theories, they have definitely changed our way of perceiving science as an adamant leviathan or, as Max Horkheimer and Theodor Adorno would have liked to have seen it, as a bastion that is not subject to any criticism of the Enlightenment apparatus of intellectual repression. Agreeing to the use of figurative metaphors, we can state that from today's point of view the process of knowledge development resembles the creation of a crystal lattice, with its numerous branches and offshoots rather than a simple series of events arranged in chronological order in the history of science understood in terms of teleology. Symbolic anthropology inscribes itself perfectly well in this picture. When we examine its unique disciplinary character, we should always consult the complexity of this trend being suspended in the anthropological thought and the social sciences. Its numerous ideological affiliations with other trends of the humanities force one to adopt the above broad view on the problem of a crystallization of the main theoretical assumptions shared by scholars who ascribe themselves into this anthropological trend.

The fact still remains, however, that presenting the scope of the research on symbolic actions, the practical operation of symbols in culture, as well as the position and forming of the stance of symbolic anthropology itself in view of trends akin to it, requires showing a relatively clear direction of development for this sub-branch; it would be an ideological way that used to be taken within the anthropological discourse in the course of time. It is because the symbolic and interpretive approach did not emerge like *deus ex machina*; neither was it a closed, intellectually autonomous anthropological school of thought unsusceptible to any inspirations. It was and it still is a trend with broad branch-related affiliations, a rich intellectual tradition and profound scientific grounds, which used to be derived from both anthropology itself and some other, sometimes extremely distant, fields of the social sciences. Thus, the narrow approach to this sub-branch as a phenomenon of purely anthropological provenance would be a considerable abuse. The reach of this trend is much wider. Symbolic anthropology is a trend that openly inscribes itself into the complex historical and scientific context, closely related to the theoretical transformations taking place inside the social sciences of the 20th-century. By contrast, the image of how that theoretical stance kept forming and how people attempted to formulate the problem of culture and society within its confines creates a colourful mosaic of inspirations that shape the scientific attitude of many well-known symbolic anthropologists.

Determining the historical moment of birth of the symbolic trend does not raise considerable doubts among contemporary anthropologists. We can speak of the existence of symbolic anthropology as a fully developed trend that has a relatively clearly defined subject of research, a consistent set of theoretical assumptions and an appropriate conceptual instrumentation since the early 1970s. Since that time, this trend, in one shape or another, has been present in anthropology until today. There is agreement on this among the very anthropologists who inscribe themselves into the symbolic trend, although, for various reasons peculiar to them, they provide disparate justifications for these time limits. At this point, the text by Sherry B. Ortner, *Theory in Anthropology since the Sixties*, can help out significantly. It is now being considered as the basic source that illustrates the view of a researcher, describing herself outright as a symbolic anthropologist, on the historical and scientific context of the development of this sub-branch. The author of *Sherpas Through Their Rituals* assumes the 1960s as a starting point for her considerations on the grounds of modern anthropological theory. In her opinion, this period was critical to the issue of forming the panorama of anthropology and the social sciences in the shape which was known towards the end of the past century, and even today. This was also the time when symbolic anthropology originated – with the formative period of this specialty, according to the American anthropologist, coming in the years 1963–1966. The concept of "symbolic anthropology" was at that time used in relation to a series of diverse indications of social thought; however, the centres of this trend were mostly located in the departments of anthropology at the American universities: the University of Chicago and the University of Cornell,[1] as well as at the British universities (particularly the units related to the so-called "Manchester school of thought"). However, it is required to

[1] The very term "symbolic anthropology" has been minted presumably by scholars with an oppositional attitude towards this trend. The very anthropologists who move in this circle have accepted it relatively late. S. Ortner, "Theory in Anthropology since the Sixties," in N. B. Dirks, G. Eley, S. Ortner (eds.), *Culture/Power/History. A Reader in Contemporary Social Theory*, Princeton 1994, p. 374.

point out straightaway (which Ortner did not mention) that neither a scientific manifesto of symbolic anthropology, nor any concise list of postulates put forward by anthropologists from this circle with regard to their own branch, have ever been formulated. In any case, the existence of such a set of theoretical assumptions for a given specialty, determined *explicite*, is an extremely rare phenomenon in contemporary science, and in the humanities in particular. What allows one today to ascertain the existence of specific discriminants of symbolic anthropology as a certain distinct trend among the social sciences is its constant attachment to searching for an answer to the question of the operation and place of symbols in culture or social life, as well as the ways of reading them. Of course, particularist answers to these questions differ from one another, depending on the perspective adopted by a given scholar and the research programme they pursue. Nevertheless, the answers always revolve around the issue of understanding culture and its particular manifestations through the analysis and interpretation of meanings that people ascribe to them.

There is also a more personal reason behind the indication of this particular lapse in the title of Ortner's article. As she herself admits, she was starting her career as an anthropologist in those years and the trends that had been topical then, exerted a considerable influence on the shaping of her later views and scientific attitude.[2] In this context, she points out the currents in the social thought of the second half of the 20th-century which have directly influenced the shaping of today's symbolic and interpretive stance. At the turn of the 1950s and 1960s, the predominant anthropological paradigms on both sides of the Atlantic were such currents as: the British structural functionalism pursued by Alfred Reginald Radcliffe-Brown and Bronisław Malinowski, the diverse varieties of evolutionism pursued in the spirit of Leslie White's and Julian Steward's thought, as well as the American psycho-cultural anthropology developed by Margaret Mead and Ruth Benedict. However, all these currents had already been perceived as insufficient in terms of theory and as intellectually outmoded at that time.

In the light of the above, certain bottom-up movements became noticeable towards the end of the 1960s, directing the social thought in

[2] Clifford Geertz adopts a similar stance in this respect. He also acknowledges that the historical moment of birth of the symbolic (interpretive) current is best defined through its institutional side. In the case of Geertz, such a caesura was bringing into existence of the School of Social Science at the Institute for Advanced Study of Princeton University at the beginning of the 1970s. C. Geertz, "School Building: A Retrospective Preface," in J. W. Scott, D. Keates (eds.), *Schools of Thought. Twenty-Five Years of Intepretative Social Science*, Princeton and Oxford 2001, p. 1.

particular to one of the aspects of researching culture – an aspect that had kept a low profile to some extent thus far towards the main current of interest expressed by scholars of the time. The change of research goals for anthropology, sociology, linguistics and social philosophy has centred on the concept of praxis (in its linguistic, cultural and social understanding), including the meanings that constitute it (in the semantic understanding). The attention of the humanities and anthropology in those years concentrated, unlike the modernist model of researching "primitive mentality" meticulously pursued thus far, on the "less rational aspects of human behaviour" as the well-known British anthropologist puts it.[3] All kinds of human behaviour and human creations related to the sphere of ideas, including its symbolic aspect, were included in the "activity" of this type. Among other things, it was because of this change that the semiotic perspective established its position in the 1960s as one of the most influential currents in the contemporary humanities, becoming even the most visible one in the realm of linguistics. Moreover, in Ortner's opinion, it was precisely the concept of "praxis" which turned out to be a specific symbol that concatenated the research challenges undertaken by the social sciences of the time into a whole. Over time, the wide range of research conducted within the scope of cultural and social *praxis* included the fields of interest peculiar to cultural ecology, political economy, structural Marxism and other currents in the humanities that raised the problem of action and used to be topical at the time. Indeed, the formation of a cohesive trend addressing these issues in the 1980s and including it under the general terms of *action theory* or *praxis theory* constituted a natural consequence of the previous trends elucidated by Ortner. According to the American anthropologist, social theories formed in this way have operated more or less since the beginning of the 1990s until today, and its contemporary object of study is constituted by all kinds of human actions embedded in the semantic context.

To adduce a short list of the most important participants in this current is as equally uncomplicated as it is to outline the time limits of symbolic anthropology. Today, it is associated mainly with the names of such researchers as: Clifford Geertz, Victor W. Turner, David M. Schneider, Mary Douglas, Sherry B. Ortner and James A. Boon.[4] While examining these names, an obvious conclusion may come to mind, namely, that this speciality has undergone the most dynamic development in academic centres in the

---

[3] R. Firth, *Symbols. Private and Public*, London 1973, p. 28.

[4] In some respect, Edmund Leach can also be included in the symbolic current, although he himself would arguably never agree with this view.

United States and Britain. One should know, however, that its range did not include large American and British universities exclusively. To a smaller extent in terms of institutional issues, although an equally intensive one, symbolic anthropology has been developed in the Scandinavian countries (the works of Ulla Britta Johansson), the Netherlands (the anthropological school of thought endorsed by the structuralist J. P. B. de Josselin de Jong) and, to a lesser extent, in France.[5]

The dislike towards structuralist reductionism manifested itself, among other things, through the turn towards culture and society being presented from the perspectives proposed by such scholars as Émile Durkheim, Max Weber, representatives of the Frankfurt school of thought, Sussane K. Langer, Talcott Parsons, Hans-Georg Gadamer, or Paul Ricoeur. The stances of these researchers were different from one another on many issues, and the fields of their interest were often very distant from one another as well. However, they were related by a sense of the inadequacy of the description of social and cultural phenomena that presumed the possibility of explaining them in a manner which would reject the important role of the semantic fabric of culture in shaping human attitudes and life choices (including the role of symbolic actions and other types of social behaviour), as well as the awareness of the complexity of the interpretive process in building social models. These postulates were not rare cases. Instead, they constituted part of a broader movement in the humanities of the period in which the symbolic approach was being formed.

Initially, sequestered voices that agitated to include interpretation in the set of tools for social sciences changed over time into a current which we could call an interpretive one from today's point of view. The so-called turn in interpretation was a phenomenon in the history of science, which had an extraordinarily powerful influence on different branches of the humanities worldwide, as well as an equally commodious set of potential objects of study. One of the revealing examples of the attitude adopted by researchers associated with this trend can be the statement of Paul Rabinow and William Sullivan, which constitutes a secondary view on the theoretical intricacies of the change in interpretation. Adopting the perspective of the over twenty years that had passed since the first symptoms of the "interpretive fever" had been noticed, they said that: "the interpretative turn refocuses atten-

---

[5] M. Des Chene, "Symbolic Anthropology," in D. Levinson, M. Ember (eds.), *Encyclopedia of Cultural Anthropology*, New York 1996, p. 1275.

tion on the concrete varieties of cultural meaning, in their particularity and complex texture, but without falling into traps of historicism or cultural relativism in their classical forms. For the human sciences both the object of investigation – the web of language, symbol, and institutions that constitutes signification – and the tools by which investigation is carried out share inescapably the same pervasive context that is the human world."[6] Setting the exploration of the "human world" as its goal, this current has included not only anthropology, but it has become a significant driving force of philosophy, sociology, psychology and, generally understood, the sciences addressing culture at the turn of the 1960s and the 1970s. One of the most important slogans spread by the representatives of this current was the deconstruction of the positivist way of thinking about culture and society. It was believed that the social sciences went into crisis, the cause of which were shortcomings in the positivist reasoning, and its consequence was a dejection about the nature of scientific explication. Some people rushed into coming to the aid of the humanities with a snappy postulate of overcoming the division of scientific cognition into its subjective and objective aspect, which was ingrained in the academic minds. The existing system, deriving from the thought of 19th-century Romanticism, in which objective and subjective analysis were contrasted with each other, was being negated. Now it is believed that these are two complementary elements of humanist interpretation.

Anthropological interpretation and ethnographic description as its appreciable outcome constitute, as Dan Sperber says today, a kind of representation.[7] Let us stop at this thesis for a while. Under the concept of representation, the French researcher understands any "thing" that replaces the object it represents during an intellectual procedure. However, the mechanism of replacing objects with other objects has to meet one condition: It should be a thing which is "adequate" to the object it replaces. Of course, there are many types of adequacy that can exist understood in this way, from the standard description of existing facts to their faithful reproduction. While making an interpretation of cultural and social phenomena, however, a researcher should bear in mind the unique character of the object of study of their own branch. Sperber also mentions the specific context of ethnographic interpretation. It is an activity embedded in the context of the ruling

[6] P. Rabinow, W. M. Sullivan, "Interpretative Turn. A Second Look," in P. Rabinow, W. M. Sullivan (eds.), *Interpretative Social Science. A Second Look,* Berkeley and Los Angeles, p. 6.

[7] D. Sperber, *On Anthropological Knowledge. Three Essays*, Cambridge 1987, p. 11.

anthropological paradigms and topical scientific trends. Here, it is also possible to distinguish several fundamental types. The most widely used stylistic measures used by anthropologists in interpretation include anecdote, gloss and generalization.[8] By remaining in the textual manner, we could state that anthropological interpretation is also often a type of indirect speech, since an anthropologist frequently employs such statements as: "according to the beliefs of the Kwakiutl tribe...," "as the priests of the Maya people believe that..." or "the Berber people claim that..." and many similar expressions.

I take the liberty to use indirect speech here in a provocative manner and adduce further theses put forward by the French scholar. In accordance with the assumptions enunciated by Dan Sperber in his work *Rethinking Symbolism*, we can state that the interpretation of the symbolic behaviour and symbolic representation of culture is deprived of legitimacy in a rationalised manner, i.e. through the formal semantic analysis (in a similar way to that in which, e.g. Claude Lévi-Strauss used to perceive it). It is because they lack semantic grounds in the sense that they do not constitute a set of logical laws and relations, unlike language with its grammatical elements, for instance. The use of linguistic methods with regard to the symbolic representation of cultural actions is an activity that assumes *a priori* their systemic rationality, i.e. the symbolic compatibility of particular actions with the rules of the social structure. However, a symbol most often eludes the conceptual targets of the researcher. It does not allow anyone to embed it into the conceptual limits of general systemic theories, nor does it submit itself to pressure, the aim of which is to transform it into a semantic ground for the rationalised forms of social behaviour. A symbol constitutes an independent cultural phenomenon of an ambivalent nature, often subjectively marked, but even more frequently subject to continual transformations arising from the internal dynamics of culture and the actions undertaken by the remaining members of society. Thus, a researcher should focus more on placing the meaning of a symbol in terms of a community which sees that very symbol in the context of a symbolic representation of the whole of their culture, rather than striving to discover its meaning which is "hidden" under that symbolic representation. In order to achieve this, the researcher is forced to go for a tool that would be adequate for this task, namely, anthropological interpretation.

By agreeing to the thesis which states that anthropological interpretation is a kind of humanist interpretation, we bestow a certain operational

[8] Ibidem, p. 14.

status on it. It is also understood in the same way within the sphere of the hermeneutic trend, the influence of which is visible in symbolic anthropology. Hermeneutic philosophy centres on the practical side of the interpretive process, where reality is shaped in the image of a text and the hermeneutic interpretation serves to provide as faithful a reflection of the world view and values presented by the author of that text as possible. Thus, the interpretation process occupies a position between the researcher and the object of study, assuming the role of a peculiar "filter" for the analyzed content. By contrast, the researcher becomes a translator of that content, translating one language of values into another. As far as anthropology is concerned, interpretation also has an epistemological potential, owing to which we strive to describe the complex system of meanings of the indigenous world in terms of its own making, or at least in terms which are as close to it as possible.

The social sciences of the second half of the 20th-century aimed at integrating various interpretive models into one cohesive research project. Towards the end of the 1960s, the fatigue of the structuralist vision and theoretical shortcomings of other similar trends awoke the need for shifting the focus of anthropological considerations to the issue of the meaning of social and cultural praxis. The American tradition of pragmatic philosophy turned out to be exceptionally helpful in determining the point of reference with regard to structuralist formalism, as well as with regard to any other empirical sectionalism. James A. Boon, the American symbolic anthropologist, also agrees with this thesis, explicitly stating that the scientific thought of Lévi-Strauss is placed in opposition to the research stances presented by those persons interested in pursuing the real incorporation of cultural interpretation into the anthropological instrumentation. Continuing his investigations, Boon promotes an idea which states that the whole of American anthropology constitutes a certain kind of aftermath of the pragmatic philosophy in this sense.[9] In its fundamental form, pragmatic philosophy strives to call into existence not a doctrine, but a research method proposal, which does not claim the right of absolute usefulness, unlike the structural method.[10] This method finds its particular application in the case of a specific object, i.e.

[9] J. Boon, *Other tribes, other scribes. Symbolic anthropology in the comparative study of cultures, histories, religions, and texts*, Cambridge 1982, p. 138. The concept of culture, as enunciated at one time by Franz Boas, the father of American anthropology, had a large impact on this state of affairs, just as the very concept's influence on the model of social sciences pursued in the United States in the 20th-century did.

[10] At this point, I have the pragmatic philosophy of William James in mind in particular.

social and cultural praxis: a phenomenon, the nature of which is as unstable, hard to define and capricious as the concept of culture is. Even Lévi-Strauss argued this in spite of the existence of fixed structures, permanent instability is a constant feature of large systems; besides, they gain their dynamism owing to that very instability. Showing the liquid character of the forms of social and cultural *praxis* has become a challenge posed to structuralism, assailed by crisis, as well as to any other reductionism which saw reason in taking social actions into consideration in themselves exclusively. The beginning of the 1970s brought something longed-for, albeit signalled long before: a breath of fresh air in the thought on this matter. One of the factors that contributed to the reinforcement of the position of the interpretive stance in those years was the increased interest in the problem of action understood in the cultural sense. The greatest merits in its scientific conceptualisation appertain to a coherent group of researchers, whose works have established the theoretical and methodological core of this trend.

The theoretical assumptions developed by Clifford Geertz constitute the most suggestive example of the interpretive approach in contemporary anthropology. They also result from the same historical and scientific processes which contributed to the formation of symbolic anthropology. The American culture researcher mentioned above is undoubtedly one of the most respected representatives of both the symbolic trend and the interpretive trend today.[11] However, he applies the concept of interpretation in several different ways, namely: 1) in claiming that interpretation of cultural phenomena constitutes the basic type of the methodological operation of the social sciences, he situates the branch he pursues among a wide circle of theoretical orientations, commonly referred to as interpretive trends; 2) he uses the term interpretation with regard to human ways of perceiving and conceptualising reality (anthropology is interpretive in character because it focuses on interpretations); 3) anthropology is also interpretive because an anthropologist interprets the interpretations made by other people by means of the cultural competence he or she possesses, and more specifically, by using his or her anthropological vocational education. Thereby, Clifford Geertz's interpretive programme constitutes a bold interdisciplinary undertaking, the aim of which is to transform cultural anthropology understood in the traditional way into a science of an understanding nature, simultaneously being part of a certain

[11] In spite of the above, he himself moves rather towards the concept of cultural hermeneutics and textualism.

general humanist vision of the world. Researching cultures (interpreting them) is the main task on which Clifford Geertz sets his sights, and the analysis of cultural discourse that takes place at the level of symbolic actions serves to show the complex character of activities commonly considered as obvious and the sense of which is not usually realised by the individuals involved in these activities. As the already mentioned Sherry Ortner stated, the most significant contribution of the author of *Local Knowledge* to the research on culture are the theses concerning its substance, formulated by that very author, as well as laying emphasis on the view as seen "from the native's point of view."[12] Both assumptions constitute the fabric of the original cultural research theory, the most fundamental part of which owes much to the works of Max Weber, Talcott Parsons, Ludwig Wittgenstein, and Ernst Cassirer.

According to Geertz, culture constitutes the focal point of social life in all of its aspects. It organises human lives, although not in the causal sense (as a pure determinant of our behaviour), but as a factor that emphasises the meaning of action, artefacts, institutions, etc. within the duration of particular cultural processes. As Geertz states in his most commented-on article *Thick Description: Toward an Interpretive Theory of Culture,* culture is a theatrically acted document, owing to which it has a public expression, i.e. it is subject to continual interpretations made by the persons who participate in it.[13] It is also not something contained in the mental or physical sphere, as the participants of the idealist and materialist dispute would like to see the problem.[14] Neither can it be considered as a self-contained and pan-organic type of reality, because it goes beyond the level of both mental processes and material needs. Its place, as Geertz claims, following the well-known ethnomethodologist Ward Goodenough, is "in the minds and hearts of men."[15] Thus, it should be understood as a set of symbolic systems and analysed through the meaning that people lend to their actions, the

---

[12] S. Ortner, "Theory in Anthropology since the Sixties," in N. B. Dirks, G. Eley, S. Ortner (ed.), *Culture/Power/History. A Reader in Contemporary Social Theory*, Princeton 1994, pp. 374–375.

[13] C. Geertz, "Thick Description: Toward an Interpretive Theory of Culture," in idem, *The Interpretation of Cultures*, New York 1973, p. 10.

[14] Geertz openly believes that a debate on the substance of culture, which emerged in the making of a dispute between the representatives of the objective and subjective stance is totally misbegotten, for none of these approaches is able to show autonomously the place culture occupies in the world view of the researched communities, Ibidem, p. 10.

[15] Ibidem, p. 11.

surrounding reality and cultural proceedings of the remaining members of the society. In such a system, researching culture is tantamount to pursuing a "concentrated description" of its practical manifestations, for the task of an anthropologist is precisely an ethnographic description of the cultural phenomena he or she experiences.

This concept, borrowed from Gilbert Ryle's thought, is the fundamental element of the theory of culture proposed by Clifford Geertz. It refers to the ethnographic praxis in its most literal sense on the one hand, and lends a new undercurrent marked with philosophical verve to the concept of ethnography on the other.[16] Pursuing anthropology is nothing else but *ethno graphōs*, that is, describing what belongs to a culturally unfamiliar order, as well as an attempt to break the barrier of semantic difference between disparate cultural systems. However, the cognition of terms of the researched culture is hedged around with specific conditions. Invoking the works of Ryle again, Geertz adduces the example of the simple activity of winking on this issue.[17] Its multiple meanings can be considered on an infinite number of semantic levels, from uncontrolled twitches to a code that is known to the sender and most often to the receiver of that signal as well. Geertz uses an analogous approach with regard to all culturally defined human actions, each of which may have a meaning that diverges from the one the researcher has just devised. By contrast, when it seems to the researcher that he or she has reached the "nature of things" again, rejecting deceptive premises suggested by the surface phenomena beforehand, they think that they will be able to determine how things are in reality right away – but it is precisely at this point when it turns out that, by looking at the object of study from a different perspective, we discover another layer of semantic relations, the existence of which we have not been aware of until now. The cultural meaning of particular phenomena appears as a never-finished project, the end of which defines itself on the horizon of the ethnographic view, but like the horizon, it is also ever-unattainable.

Geertz's reasoning in favour of the interpretive theory of culture finds explicit reflection in his anthropological practice during the research he conducted in Morocco and Indonesia. It was here that he witnessed signif-

[16] It is worth knowing that before getting interested in cultural anthropology, Clifford Geertz studied philosophy at the University of Antioch, and thus his education with regard to philosophy can be treated as another factor that has shaped his views as an anthropologist.

[17] At this point, I take the liberty to omit a detailed description of the whole demarcation between the possible meanings of that activity, extensively quoted by Geertz.

icant processes of cultural change that made Geertz aware of the liquidity and the possibility of simultaneous co-existence of several interpretations of the same cultural phenomena. Thus, being aware of the limits of his profession, he holds to a view that the language of traditionally understood anthropology is unable to convey in full the anthropological field experience. The task of the picturesque imagery, characteristic of later works by Clifford Geertz, is to break that very resistance of ethnographic matter and bring the theoretical fabric of his anthropological thinking closer to the object of interpretive analysis. However, this procedure does much more as well. It brings interpretive anthropology closer to literature, i.e. to creating specific types of cultural narratives that have their unique style, language and a resource of metaphors.

The theoretical assumptions of Clifford Geertz, maintained in the manner of the Weberian concept of a network of meanings that are simultaneously created by humans and shape their representation of the world, primarily revolve around the problems of the unique character of an anthropological description of culture. The assumption of the need for researching culture "from the native's point of view" has a significant role in this regard. It has been enunciated in an article with a symptomatic title: *From the Native's Point of View. On the Nature of Anthropological Understanding* contained in the work *Local Knowledge. Further essays within the scope of interpretive anthropology*, where arguments in favour of this concept can be put in the following way: anthropology researches human cultural convictions situated in the systemic context. By contrast, interpretive anthropology is science that addresses the anchoring of these very convictions, world views and the "ethos" of a given culture, in the local network of meanings, unceasingly negotiated by its representatives. Invoking the demarcation between the concepts that are "close to" and "distant from experience," developed by Heinz Kohut at one time, Clifford Geertz moves towards the thesis that an anthropologist has to take the above context into consideration in their research, based on the direct character of the field work. As Geertz says: "the trick is to figure out what the devil they think they are up to."[18]

The vision of culture presented by Clifford Geertz is in a close and undisguised relation to the theses of Talcott Parsons. Another anthropologist, whose works reveal similar sources of inspiration, is David M. Schneider.

[18] C. Geertz, "From the Native's Point of View. On the Nature of Anthropological Understanding," in idem, *Local Knowledge. Further essays within the scope of interpretive anthropology*, New York 2000, p. 58.

Just like Geertz, Schneider is also regarded as a leading representative of the American faction of symbolic anthropology and, just like the author of *The Interpretation of Cultures*, he expresses a view that the substance of cultural phenomena of any kind are made up of the symbolic relations that constitute them. In the "manifesto" of the symbolic approach, published for the first time in 1968, under the title *American Kinship. A Cultural Account*, Schneider states that: "certainly culture is in one sense a regularity of human behavior, and as such is quite objective and quite real. But this does not mean that any observable, definable, demonstrable regularity of human behavior is culture. Neither does it mean that culture can be directly inferred from any regular pattern of human behavior."[19] This work constitutes a result of Schneider's cooperation with Raymond Firth and in the conception of both scholars it was to be part of a larger comparative study of the American and British systems of family ties.[20] In his work, the American anthropologist included the foundations of his theory of kinship, the most widely commented fragment of which turned out to be the thesis which stated that as far as the issue of establishing kinship relations is concerned, it is not the real biological relations that are important, but symbolic relations, i.e, culturally established terms of kinship.[21] In such a system, kinship relations constitute a self-governing cultural system which, in the case of American society, manifests itself through creating relations of a kin nature with regard to persons who are not necessarily close to one another in terms of genetics. The American culture establishes two separate orders of things on this issue, namely, it makes a distinction between "the natural law" ("the Order of Nature") and "the statutory law" ("the Order of Law"). Schneider argues that the Americans, when talking about the natural law and the statutory law, use concepts that symbolically refer to "blood" and "relation" in the first case, or to "love" in the second case. An important element of these conceptual procedures is the symbolic representation of a sexual intercourse, which cements them, an example of which is constituted by the relations between husband and wife (based on the statutory

[19] D. Schneider, *American Kinship. A Cultural Account*, Chicago and London 1980, p. 5.

[20] However, Schneider ascertained that Firth's work was overly sociological and then he withdrew from the collaborative project.

[21] In other words, our kin is the one whom we regard as such. The use of the terms "uncle" and "aunt" with regard to close acquaintances of the parents may serve as an example here.

law) or between parents and children (the natural law that emphasises the taboo of incest).

The scientific resonance accompanying the sexual aspect of cultural relations, emphasised by David Schneider in his work *American Kinship*, coincided with the beginning of the sexual revolution which fell on the 1960s and the social expression of which was provided by such factors as, e.g. the counterculture movement or the release of Alfred Kinsey's report earlier on. The interest which Schneider's theses awoke among the scholars of the time was understandably marked by the influence of the events mentioned above, but the main axis of debate on the theses put forward in *American Kinship* turned out to be his concept of culture. Unlike Geertz, who moved rather towards the development of an interpretive and symbolic concept of anthropology itself in his works, David Schneider was headed towards creating a specific theory of culture. The influence of Parsons's thought on Schneider's anthropology mentioned earlier found its expression in the underlining of the systemic view it pursues. In his article *Notes toward a Theory of Culture*, Schneider explicates this stance, claiming that culture cannot be reduced to a system of a different type, due to which the research of cultural phenomena in their own terms becomes possible.[22] It is an irreducible analytical construct and at the same time pursuing cultural studies deprived of any reference to a broader social theory is pointless. Thus, the basic objects of symbolic analysis are particular forms of human behaviour. Researching them is based on several types of abstractions, the most important of which are standards and culture.[23] They are comparable abstractions of the social and cultural order. Schneider sees the place of culture in the shaping of social actions that constitute the semantic activity of humans. However, social action requires the existence of a common level of understanding culture, commonly shared codes of social communication and including generalized relations between particular elements of culture in them. The observable deed of action can be considered on two levels at least. First, it may establish social norms; second, abstractions determine the norms for a certain class of actions.

---

[22] D. M. Schneider, "Notes Toward a Theory of Culture," in K. Basso, H. A. Shelby (ed.), *Meaning in Anthropology*, Albuquerque 1976, p. 197.

[23] Under the concept of abstraction, David Schneider understands "an analytically defined operation that is applicable to, and can be drawn from, observations of behavior." Ibidem, p. 198.

The model of culture called into existence by David Schneider is based on the assumption that there are its two fundamental functions – the integrative function and the generative function. The integrative function involves what Parsons called "pattern maintenance." This means that culture constitutes a factor that unites particular fragments of social order into a whole that is comprehensible for the members of the society. The other function of culture is the generative one due to a shift which it makes in the position of culture – from the holistic and systemic vision towards a state in which its changes, modifications or innovations become the main reference point for the continuance of the society. The thesis about the significant influence of these functions on social action inspired Schneider to enunciate his views on culture in an exceptionally precise way. He says that culture is a "system of symbols and meanings," simultaneously being an important determinant of cultural action.[24] However, a statement that the issue here is some kind of cultural determinism proves deceptive. Schneider focuses his attention on answering the question about the meaning of the symbolic categorisation of cultural phenomena and, ultimately, on obtaining the image of the meaning of these categories for the system of culture understood in terms of particularism. As he said himself in *American Kinship*, his goal is to show American categories of kinship first "as a cultural system, as a system of symbols, and not as a »description« at any other level."[25]

The vital interest of British anthropology has always aimed at research on the substance of society, its structure, the organization of social relations and the position of institutions in shaping the general social system. The concept of culture, so important for American anthropology, has usually played a secondary role in the works by British scholars; sometimes people even strove to avoid it, an example of which can be the attitude presented by Radcliffe-Brown, who claimed that the use of the term "culture" in the natural social sciences is groundless. The British anthropological tradition has been embedded in a current, the limits of which are determined mainly by the works of Durkheim, Malinowski and French structuralists. Sources of inspiration of this type were peculiar to British anthropologists of the end of the 1960s as well. Just like their American colleagues, they moved towards researching the semantic grounds of society and over time they contributed to the creation of the British variety of symbolic anthropology.

[24] Ibidem, p. 198.

[25] D. M. Schneider, *American Kinship. A Cultural Account*, Chicago and London 1980, p. 18.

This group should include, first of all, Victor W. Turner and Mary Douglas, who undertook to present the dependencies taking place between society and the symbolic dimension of social action.

The anthropological thought of Victor W. Turner is marked by a peculiar approach to the problem of the symbolic representation of social and cultural actions. The main point of Turner's symbolic analysis is social process understood in terms of social drama. The task of theatre imagery employed by Turner in his most important works is to emphasise the influence of cultural representation on the trend, as well as on the practical manifestations of social action. Turner's early studies centred on researching social structure and its continuance over time, an issue which has been abandoned in subsequent works in favour of the problem of the meaning of rites. The organization of society is dynamically marked, whereas the social structure is ceaselessly tormented by internal conflicts and strain. In order to remedy the break of mutual bonds, society employs appropriate mechanisms which are to prevent its disintegration. The concept of *social drama* created by Turner conveys mechanisms of this type perfectly well, simultaneously indicating the manipulations which the social symbolic representation is subject to. The conviction about the sequential character of the social process, derived from reading *Les rites de passage* by Arnold van Gennep, directed Turner towards the research on the symbolic representation of ritualised forms of social action.[26] In his work *The Forest of Symbols. Aspects of Ndembu Ritual* he expresses his views on the functioning of symbols and the importance of the social behaviour of people. Complementing and transforming the triadic division of subsequent stages of the rites of passage presented by van Gennep, Turner drew particular attention to the meaning of the liminal stage.

The concept of liminality is one of the interesting research theories proposed by Victor W. Turner. He utilised the division of the rites of passage (into the stages of: exclusion/separation, marginalisation, inclusion/aggregation) developed by van Gennep in order to show the important role of the marginalisation stage for the continuance of the social structure. It

---

[26] It is worth knowing that the interest Victor W. Turner expressed in the achievements of van Gennep was accidental to a large extent. During a forced stopover in Hastings in 1963, Turner found a copy of *The rites of passage* in the local library and reading it resulted in the classic essay: "Betwixt and Between: The Liminal Period in Rites de Passage." See M. Deflem *Ritual,* "Anti-Structure, and Religion: A Discussion of Victor Turner's Processual Symbolic Analysis," *Journal for the Scientific Study of Religion*, 30 (1)/1991, pp. 1–25.

consists in the temporary *anomie* of the existing structure and passage to the interstructural stage of *communitas*.[27] Generally speaking, *communitas* is a specific stage at which the existing social relations become reversed and all the constituents of the old order are put in semantic opposition with regard to their "normal" place in the system. Turner extended the opposition structure/*communitas*, which he outlined, to other aspects of social life, as well. Namely, he claimed that the dialectic model of the process in which two social orders contend with each other can be successfully cross-referred to the sphere of basic social relations. Thus, *communitas* was to be reflected by a community of individuals – undifferentiated and egalitarian to a large extent, whereas the concept of structure constitutes the reflection of the hierarchical system of positions peculiar to differentiated communities.

As a witness of the violent changes taking place in the 1960s in Western societies, Turner ventured an attempt to apply the *communitas* theory to the hippie movement, which was emerging at that time. Owing to the differentiation of this concept into three basic types (existential, normative and ideological *communitas*), he retraced the process of shaping these types within the sphere of that movement. The structure of the hippie communities turned out to be subject to continual and oriented transformations – from a spontaneous movement, to planned actions, to the formation of the ideology of pacifism and free love. The issue of the processuality of social life raised during the research had found its more profound expression previously in the work *The Forest of Symbols*. Field studies conducted by Turner among the Ndembu people in north-west Zambia indicated the problem of the instability of the social structure, as well as a conflict. Taking the model of social organisation based on the "structure of positions" as a starting point, Turner addressed the question about the grounds for sudden outbursts of collective discontent and the questioning of the existing order. As he stated much later, in his work *Dramas, Fields, and Metaphors. Symbolic Action in Human Society*, the most distinctive feature of the social life of the Ndembu people was a constant pursuit of conflict, i.e. social drama.[28] We similarly face the situation of social drama during the pending social process, more specifically when the interests and attitudes of both groups and individuals are laid in obvious opposition.[29] Then the units of the social

[27] Turner took this term from the works by Paul Goodman.

[28] V. Turner, *Dramas, Fields, and Metaphors. Symbolic Action in Human Society*, Ithaca and London 1974, p. 35.

[29] Ibidem, p. 35.

process, which can be isolated and captured in ethnographic description, constitute themselves.

Turner employed the processual approach towards the issue of social structure in the majority of his works and it has simultaneously become the foundation for the model of anthropology postulated by this British scholar. He championed the *anthropology of experience* and, in a broader perspective, the *anthropology of performance*. He assumed that the "major genres of cultural performance (from ritual to theater to film) and narration (from myth to the novel) not only originate in the social drama, but also continue to draw meaning and force from the social drama."[30] By invoking Wilhelm Dilthey, he made a bold conjunction of the philosophical concept of the structure of experience with the conceptual apparatus of anthropology. The anthropology of experience was expected to turn out to be a tool employed in researching cultural phenomena for their rooting in the existential, sometimes even emotional, aspect of social life. The best research material for the anthropological profession understood in this way are rites, theatre performances, ballads, epic tales, or operas – which convey the image of a given culture far better than the customs of its members, understood in a narrow sense. Turner saw this problem in the same way as Dewey and Dilthey saw society – as a pulsating and rhythmic co-existence, full of cleavages and reintegration. By emphasising the importance of the symbolic representation accompanying the ritualised forms of dealing with the crisis, he strove to indicate specific rules that regulate the creation of the social process and shape structural changes. However, he did not forget about the place occupied by the anthropologist, as well as the influence that the presence of an observer exerts on the object of analysis. As he himself ascertained: "of all the human sciences and studies anthropology is most deeply rooted in the social and subjective experience of the inquirer."[31]

In spite of the close intellectual contact with academic centres in the United States, Victor W. Turner remained a British anthropologist.[32] The so-called Manchester school affiliation made his works bear the mark of

---

[30] V. Turner, *On the Edge of the Bush. Anthropology as Experience*, Tucson 1985, p. 201.

[31] V. Turner, "Dewey, Dilthey and Drama: An Essay in the Anthropology of Experience," in V. W. Turner, E. M. Bruner (eds.), *The Anthropology of Experience*, Tucson 1986, p. 33.

[32] In 1963, Turner accepted a position at Cornell University and then he also worked at the University in Chicago and the University of Virginia between 1968 and 1977.

that theoretical and methodological tradition. Turner himself also admitted the enormous influence that the works of Max Gluckman exerted on him. However, the case of Victor W. Turner is not representative of the faction of the symbolic current pursued in the United Kingdom to such an extent as are the works of another, equally well-known figure of British anthropology. Of course, we are talking here of Mary Douglas, whose studies within the scope of the symbolic representation of impurity and risk constitute an excellent example of the grafting and transforming of the assumptions of structuralism on the British soil.

The book *Purity and Danger*, published for the first time in 1966, is a model example of the British anthropological structuralism of the 1960s. The work contains an analysis of the symbolic representation accompanying religious beliefs concerning the sphere of impurity and taboo, focussing on showing this problem in view of creating specific world view concepts. Remaining under the influence of Franz Steiner, Douglas holds the view that every culture creates its own world. It is a universe of values that are placed in a holistic context of meanings; in this case the "dangers possible in any given universe [of culture – J. D.]."[33] The society constitutes a structure that stands in the centre of its own universe. This structure affects the members of the community both adversely and positively. However, it is not placed in a semantic vacuum and it does not create a neutral *continuum* free from conflicts. The society is subject to continual influence from the outside and what does not belong to the native system is treated as hostile and as a source of potential risk. The mechanism of exclusion from culture and clamping specific sanctions in view of phenomena that go beyond the system of ruling social values translates into a symbolic transfer outside the borders of the social structure. In the opinion of Mary Douglas, collective convictions concerning separation, purity and punishment for overstepping social norms do have a function of systematising the unordered experience. Social order is created only through the introduction of a demarcation between such categories as, e.g. inside/outside, up/down or male/female. However, the above theses do not set the concept of the symbolic representation of the taboo beyond the historical process. A significant element of the symbolic theory of Mary Douglas is taking into consideration the factor of change that affects all types of cultural representations.

[33] M. Douglas, *Purity and Danger. An Analysis of Concepts of Pollution and Taboo*, London and New York 2002, p. 5.

In her early works, Mary Douglas laid emphasis on the structural dimension of cultural symbolic representation, which has also become visible in the work *Natural Symbols. Explorations in Cosmology* from 1970, being a continuation of strands raised earlier in *Purity and Danger*. Making a certain turn in methodology towards branches different than anthropology (especially towards the sociology of religion, in particular the one pursued by Durkheim), Douglas undertook to conduct an analysis of religious symbols from the point of view of their emotional influence on people's lives, as well as the cultural strategies constructed by those people based on these symbols. In this sense, *Natural Symbols* constitute a certain kind of defence of the stance developed in *Purity and Danger,* a defence, it should be added, not only full of passion, but also well-argued.[34] The British anthropologist argues that the attitude of a human towards nature can be expressed only through symbolic relations, i.e. the conceptual relation between the spheres of nature and culture. The rejection of the comparative method results in the contextualization of symbolic phenomena becoming a necessary condition for their scientific description. However, embedding the meaning of a symbol in the semantic structure of a given culture prevents one from calling a certain pan-human resource of basic symbols into existence, such as symbols that refer to physiological issues which are common to all people, after all. The social sciences have considered this problem for a long time and the majority of scholars – contemporaries of Douglas – firmly persisted with this stance. *Natural Symbols* are a work, the aim of which is to break that resistance and give way to a slightly different view. According to Douglas, the community of natural symbols is a set of ways of establishing communication between one another by means of symbols, in other words by means of symbolic structures, which are constant in all communities. These theses, which are close to the assumptions made by Lévi-Strauss, constitute the basis for the symbolic theory proposed by Douglas. Extending them in her later works onto the issues of the operation of institutions or the problems of the symbolic categorization of phenomena of contemporary culture, she expressed her research interest developed at the University of Oxford. The vision of society and culture present in the works of Mary Douglas remains in close relation to the British tradition of the social sciences, which significantly contributed to the formations of symbolic anthropology in this country.

---

[34] R. Fardon, *Mary Douglas: An Intellectual Biography*, London and New York 1999, p. 104.

The phenomenon of a strong aspiration for the transformation of the social sciences has become increasingly visible since the 1960s, and the aftershock of the dissension taking place between disparate stances in anthropology, sociology and philosophy resonated across scientific works of the time. As I have mentioned above, one of the most important trends which the humanities followed in those years was the interpretive current. Its consequence and derivative was the emergence of symbolic anthropology at the beginning of the 1970s. In its early form, symbolic anthropology utilized the rich research tradition developed by scholars interested in the issues of the semantic aspect of human existence. Creating the framework for the interpretation project, this current never constituted an anthropological school of thought understood in traditional terms; it did not have narrowly understood institutions, or a programme. What it did have, however, was a coherent group of its protagonists, who indicated new trends in cultural analysis, transferred the object of anthropological study beyond cultural phenomena understood *per se*, as well as indicated new tools for social studies. The formation of symbolic anthropology was a long and sometimes ambiguous process. Essentially, this state of affairs has continued until today, effecting such trends as the theory of performance or textualism. At present, some of the scholars who have created under the paradigm of symbolic anthropology move away from their previous theses, whereas others reinforce them. The fact still remains, however, that many of the most well-known figures of this trend evolved towards an analytical view on the concept of the interpretation and practical manifestations of cultural symbolism. Thus, one could say that despite several visible discrepancies, slightly dissimilar stances and the difference of views adopted by Geertz, Turner, or Douglas, symbolic anthropology has been concordant with regard to one issue. Both culture and society are dependent on the symbolic representation constructed by humans – it is that representation that creates motivations for their actions, as well as values and world views. Seen from this perspective, an undeniable contribution of the symbolic current to contemporary anthropology was the creation of the grounds for the research on the semantic (and not only semantic) aspect of culture.

The main objects of research in symbolic studies are human ways of understanding and interpreting their surroundings, including the actions and statements of other members of society. Such forms of interpretation share a common system of meanings (the level of understanding for cultural symbolic representation), thus creating culture. Culture, as David Schneider expressed it emphatically, is an independent system of meanings, constructed in the shape of a text, the basic elements of which are the symbols and rites of crucial importance for a given culture. Cultural actions are its language. The cultural convictions underlying these actions may seem unclear when we examine them as existing reality. They gain their expression only after they have been located within a wider symbolic system, similarly to the particular constituents of a sentence which create a consistent whole only after providing an appropriate layout for them. Symbolic action is rich in metaphors and analogies; moreover, it is one of its basic properties. In order to understand the purpose of symbolic actions, it is required to refer them to other types of human activity, owing to which they gain their proper meaning.[35]

The contextualization of the cultural activity of humans is not only one of the most important tools used within the sphere of symbolic anthropology. It is also an important component in theoretical considerations. Taking into account the fact that there are many ways of reading culture, which result from various points of view and perspectives, is a necessary stage of the interpretation process. When interpreting social institutions, systems of kinship or art, it is required to get into one's own place in this process; it is as if one should stand aside, yet simultaneously remain aware of their rooting in culture. As I have striven to prove in this text, symbolic anthropology may be deemed a separate trend within cultural anthropology due to its strong link with the postulates of the turn in interpretation and other symbolic trends, the formation of a more or less clear stance with regard to the problem of culture and cultural action, as well as the undertaking of research on a specific object of anthropological analysis. I believe, however, that this trend can be treated not only in terms of a sub-branch of anthropology. Owing to the works of Clifford Geertz and Victor W. Turner, symbolic anthropology also shows some tendencies towards the shaping of a clear scientific attitude. This attitude is marked by a strenuous desire to convey the indigenous world view, values and norms, in the same way in which the subjects themselves see them. For symbolic anthropology the postulate of researching culture "from the point of view of the indigene" is a symptomatic determinant of its theoretical assumptions. It has been exhaustively presented in the works of Geertz, but the signals related to it can also be seen in the anthropology of Bronisław Malinowski.

---

[35] J. Dolgin, D. S. Kemnitzer, D. M. Schneider (eds.), *Symbolic Anthropology. A Reader in the Study of Symbols and Meanings*, New York 1977, p. 43.

Chapter 2

Teaching the *other*. Anthropology of education in the perspective of European cultural dilemmas

While discussing European culture, in the first place one usually thinks of such terms as heritage, high culture, cultural elites or cultural values. This highly monolithic and ethnocentric view of the European culture derives from its classic definitions, reaching back to the ancient Greek and Roman philosophical traditions and conceptual figures. As it was pointed out by many Ancient philosophers, culture in the occidental philosophy is what we are supposed to gain through learning and self-perfection. There is a certain level of culture one has to achieve to call oneself a civilized human. Hence, the definition of culture becomes both processual and teleological, highlighting and justifying a specific direction of human existence and basing itself upon scientific inquiries about the surrounding world. According to these enquiries, the human individual is somehow directed towards elitist cultural activities such as philosophy, art or other forms of aesthetics. Such a definition of culture is revealed by, for example, Cicero in his writings. In the Middle Ages culture was associated with religious values and theological disputes regarding the meaning of the human existence, whereas Christian culture was perceived as God's gift given to man. Consequently, man was obliged to cherish culture by keeping his cultural values pure.

The construction of culture was at that time a product of the divine order, and so too was the social structure. Therefore, any attempt to raise the issue of the category of difference was doomed to failure since a predominant cultural pattern had to be maintained by all possible means, including direct violence against those who tried to overthrow their rulers, question the position of the Roman Catholic Church or disobey the existing paradigm. A growing number of religious conflicts spreading throughout Europe highlighted the differentiation of the European societies mostly in terms of faith and confession. Paradoxically, the Protestant revolution resulted in the strengthening of the religious ties. In the book entitled "The Protestant ethics and the spirit of capitalism" Max Weber claims that the cultural ideology on which the social actions undertaken by the English Puritans in the 16th-century was based, contributed directly to the emergence of the modern European institutions and society known in its contemporary form.[1]

Throughout the ages the European societies have established a certain (durable) tradition in their cultural discourse. This tradition consists mostly of a centralized core of the cultural ideas, all of which are the products of the historical processes taking place through the ages in the Western context of Christianity. The emergence of the social sciences in the 19th-century did not change much in this matter. The evolutionist and positivist view of culture prevailed in the European thought throughout the 19th-century. What is more, it remains popular today. In this cultural model our own culture has to be considered as the most efficient, developed and modern variant of all the cultures existing in the world. Sir James George Frazer, a classic evolutionist, argues that the key factor in the cultural development is the worldview shared by people, which drives them in their actions. This shift from the idea to agency is essential in understanding how western societies have conceptualized what is culturally different. The cultural *other* had to be conquered in order to be located into the rational frames of the western positivistic philosophy. Culture was supposed to be implemented into those societies which did not share the European view. This perfectly corresponds to Frazer's view, who states in his book entitled "The Golden Bough" that being savage means to differ in one's thoughts and actions from the scientific point of view.[2] Therefore, non-Europeans had to learn how to think and behave in the European manner.

However, there was a significant problem in teaching those abilities to the "primitive" tribes in Africa and people in other parts of the world. The

[1] See M. Weber, *The Protestant ethic and the spirit of capitalism*, New York 2001.

[2] J. G. Frazer, *The golden bough. The study in magic and religion*, New York 2002.

main obstacle was the difference in the worldviews presented by Europeans and non-Europeans. This ideological gap could only be covered by something that could explain to westerners how the cultural *other* thinks, so that his behavior could be predicted in a rational manner and thus he could be controlled in a political sense. As on many occasions in history, direct force had been applied for this reason. Moreover, the colonial involvement of the Europeans in the second half of the 19th-century shows how this policy of direct compulsion towards those who differ functioned in an educational sense. The establishment of the colonial rule and colonial schooling system also reveals a scientific paradigm. Social sciences were applied to provide the theories for the construction of primitive societies, their religions and beliefs, political and economic life and many other fields of human existence. Thus, culture was defined mostly in terms of the Western civilization. Religion, law, political power, art and other phenomena were taken into account to establish the standards set by the colonizers. Their interest lay upon a deep cultural change of those who looked and acted differently. The acculturation process was perceived as a necessity – a civilizatory mission that was to undoubtedly result in *others*' becoming members of a modern society. British colonial schools in Africa or India, the so-called Indian Boarding Schools in the United States or the missionary schools in South and Central America, all shared the belief that the savage should be converted into a being that was recognizable as one of us.

In all these cases the cultural inclusion was the main argument in the construction of the current schooling policies. Educational institutions such as public schools, universities and private institutions were designed to maintain the cultural integrity of the national community. The boarding schools in North America set up in the second half of the 19th-century to educate the Indians in the United States and Canada serve as a good example of the early nationalistic discourse in the context of the education of natives.[3] Such schools were perceived by their creators as one of the most significant tools in the acculturation process of the Native Americans. They were a model solution for the growing problem of the cultural differentiation of the American society at the end of the century. Therefore, the boarding schools model was approved by many as a part of a broader assimilation policy towards not just Indians, but also the growing flow of immigrants reshaping the

[3] See C. F. Trafzer, J. A. Keller, L. Sisquoc (eds.), *Boarding school blues. Revisiting American Indian educational experiences*, Winnipeg 2006.

ethnic and cultural face of America at the beginning of the 20th-century. It resulted in the fact that the issue of multiculturalism was first raised in the United States in the 1920s and 1930s as the American society changed in its ethnic structure. These processes taking place in America might serve as an example of how educational institutions function in a specific cultural environment where the category of difference is taken into account as an integral part of the reality surrounding us.

Today, Europeans experience a similar shift in their cultural identity. The Schengen Agreement opened borders and resulted in an increased mobility of people across the continent, changing the traditional view of nations and states as closed units. The presence of migrants in European societies as well as the processes of social change which occurred in Europe after 1945 have contributed to a more liberal perception of *otherness* and cultural diversity in general. On the other hand, many inhabitants of the Old Continent refuse to accept the fact of this transgression, still expressing the idea of a monolithic European civilization placed among other (less developed) civilizations. Some may take it for granted but the phenomena occurring in the European context nowadays provide us with some striking examples of a specific cultural discourse which affects our definition of culture today and which is very similar to the American discussions on national identity mentioned above. The colonial past of the European continent, massive migration into Europe from other parts of the world and globalization processes are only a small number of the problems constructing that discourse. These examples show a clear disruption in this traditional and homogenous view of what belongs to culture and what does not. A symbolic crack in the European identity is seen as a crisis situation. As in many other cases, the emergence of a polarized worldview shared by many Europeans (where the old cultural order is being placed against non-European extremism) was only a matter of time.

The controversy raised in 2001 by Oriana Falacci's article and later by the book "The rage and the pride" illustrates such a worldview. This Italian author and journalist attempts to show that the world today is falling to pieces.[4] These fragments of reality affect all of us in the sense that we participate in this process of decay. Fallaci's book points out the main reasons for this situation, which are associated with the erosion of our European cultural pride. According to Fallaci, the lack of cultural values, or the absence of tradition or a liberal approach toward the assimilation of migrants, are just

[4] See O. Fallaci, *The rage and the pride*, New York 2002.

some of them. Her standpoint and the reaction of the readers (who enthusiastically welcomed the book) show that contemporary European societies are tending to accept a radical turn in cultural and political ideology more readily than they did in the past. Certainly, this is just an exaggeration of some voices heard today in the European cultural discussion. On the other hand, these voices are rather loud and determined.

The latest massacre in Norway has had a deep impact on the way the cultural landscape in the old continent is viewed. After Breivik's bloody action, religious and cultural fundamentalism is no longer the attribute of the *other* since it took place within the European landscape and is deeply grounded on what is seen as a set of the so-called authentic European values. Furthermore, the perpetrator considered his deed as an extreme, but necessary act of self-defence against the growing stream of cultural and ideological *otherness* flowing into the authentically European field of the Christian tradition. Breivik's testimony has raised an important question. Being members of the modern European societies, are we still ready to accept the *other* among us? Is it possible to co-exist with people whose way of living is not accepted by us or, even worse, whose culture we despise? Were the ideas achieved by the changes in the 1960s just as a daydream cherished by a few liberals? These and other questions are the key issues Europe has to answer nowadays when dealing with the category of cultural *otherness*. It might be obvious that we tend to face these problems through the ideological glasses of politics. However, it is also important to look closely at the role the social sciences play in providing answers to them.

The scientific discipline which deals with culture and cultural *otherness* is widely associated with various forms of anthropological thought, whereas anthropological encounters with the cultural *other* remain a central figure in the discipline's dictionary. The category of cultural difference itself has made a long-lasting career in this field of knowledge ever since the beginnings of the anthropological reflection on man as a culturally-defined being. Starting from Herodot's *opus magnum* "History" one may follow a long path of attempts to picture the *other* as a lacanian mirror reflection of ourselves (just like in the writings of Herodot), or as an exotic exhibit in the collection of cultural curiosities (like, for example, in the evolutional concepts of James Frazer) held by the man of the West in his museums of natural history. Anthropologists used to think that differences enrich the world. They liked to present themselves as "agents of love" who distributed the knowledge on man in his various cultural forms of living. From the very beginning of anthropology cultural particularism was taken for granted as a natural source of the ethnographic data. The *other* was always someone whose ways of living remained far from what used to be perceived as our own lifestyle. It does not make a difference whether one speaks about a geographical distance, like in the case of exotic tribes living on the peripheries of our know world, or a social difference discussed in the context of the European folklore in the 19th-century. In both cases anthropology provided us with a fascinating picture of exotic rituals, patterns of behavior or customs which revealed a striking difference from what was known by us in our own cultural backyard. The more exotic the anthropological inquires were, the more we wanted to get into the middle of the story. Gradually, an anthropological storytelling became a fashionable occupation among both professional scholars and people who had no ethnographic competencies at all. The explosion of interest in studying anthropology and conducting more or less anthropological fieldwork had its peak in the late 1960s due to the counter-cultural tendencies in the West. Accordingly, many educators tried to apply the anthropological theories and methods in their own praxis in schools, especially when dealing with the problem of cultural diversity within the student groups. The distance between the teacher and the student became cultural. Consequently, being a cultural phenomenon, it had to be minimized to achieve educational success.

On the other hand, cultural distance is also a kind of a troublesome factor, to paraphrase the title of the book by James Clifford.[5] The history of anthropology provides us with the examples of how anthropologists deal with the problem of culture and their own lack of cognitive resources to "think like the Other." The publication of Bronisław Malinowski's diaries is considered to be a turning point in the idealistic view of the essence of the anthropological fieldwork. Being in opposition to his previous works, his diary is a reflection on the Europeans living among exotic *others*. In his own words the author disliked the object of the study, illustrating the worst prejudice against non-Europeans in his argumentation and showing his own methodological and existential frustration.[6] A historic paradox, many Trobriand islanders as it is depicted by Malinowski in his books are educated in their own cultural traditions.

[5] See J. Clifford, *The Predicament of Culture: Twentieth-Century Ethnography, Literature, and Art*, Cambridge 1988.

[6] On the other hand, Malinowski's views may be considered as typical for westerners at that time and not shocking at all from his perspective.

Thus, the work of this Polish-British anthropologist might serve as a good example of a deep methodological problem which is specific for the ethnographic research and is also present in the educational sphere. In many ways the description of cultural *otherness* differs from our understanding of it and of our acting (as a group or an individual) in the situation where the *other* is not just present but he interacts with us on a daily basis. Experiencing *otherness* is here an act of self-identification by emphasizing differences. The main issue is the following question: How can we construct our own identity in a culturally diversified world without producing the mechanisms to marginalize the *other*? Is a culturally neutral education possible at all or do educational systems tend to unify students in a cultural sense?

Without any doubt, the concept of *otherness* is also a central point in the modern educational debates, where it is raised with the issue of multiculturalism and multicultural education. This specific educational and political strategy is implemented in the context of a dramatically changing level of diversity among student groups in those European countries whose systems allow to express people's cultural identity in a pluralistic manner. Therefore, the multicultural society is a model of the simultaneously pluralistic and liberal system where every single group is given access to the cultural mainstream in the name of democracy. Multicultural education in Europe is based upon the fact, or rather upon the assumption, that European societies are pluralistic in their core ideas, whereas the set of those ideas might (actually) be as diverse as the multicultural classroom in the contemporary schools in Germany, Sweden or Great Britain can be. This assumption takes us to the point where today's cultural diversity of once homogenous European societies is celebrated as one of these ideas and it is put in the center of our discussion over the future shape of our continent.

For a long time the idea of multiculturalism and multicultural education was one of the prevailing elements in the discussion around the concept of *otherness*. Cultural otherness was also slowly gaining recognition in relation to the more subtle criteria of difference. These criteria could be made by the category of sex, age, political affiliation etc. Those fields were the factor for further diversification and social stratification. To paraphrase Bourdieu, social distinction is related to the cultural capital and the *habitus* we are given by the society. Our own creation of the social and cultural field of agency is in this case conditioned by the cultural values and ideas we share with other people. No matter whether these values and ideas are an object of conflict or an element stabilizing the social structure – they are being expressed through means given us by culture itself.

In the light of these remarks, multicultural education seems to be rather a question of a processual approach. A cultural change is here a part of the particular system as well an element of the contact between various cultural systems and the phenomena of the diffusion of selected elements of those systems. The ambiguous character of such phenomena is paradoxically not always a source of destabilization. It shakes the foundations of the cultural system only if the system's integration as the main goal set by people who live within the system is taken for granted. Social praxis shows us clearly that not all participants in social life are interested in maintaining this narrowly understood type of integration. People tend to follow their own interests within the given cultural field, which is also conditioned by the historical process it produced. In this sense, the flow of cultural content within the system and between different systems contributes to the dynamics of diversification in a very structural way. The structure of norms, values, aesthetics and beliefs is enriched by new elements which sometimes are treated as alien towards the old system. The discussion on the tradition and on history emerges almost as a natural cause of this process. Although constant reshaping and transforming of the cultural structure is a process we witness in every possible sphere of our existence, it also takes place at various speeds. In some spheres it may bring no changes at all, and in other spheres changes can be big enough to be recognized as a cultural revolution. This situation triggers a wide discussion on the transmission of traditional ideas and in this field education becomes highly relevant.

Current European educational debates may seem as diverse as the educational systems they relate to, but we are still able to emphasize significant points of reference common for all of them. In the western part of the continent, in countries like France, Spain or Italy, education is presented as a field of systematic actions for the inclusion of all people who are excluded in the fields different to education. No matter if one speaks about ethnic minorities, children from poor families, or children affected by other forms of exclusion, most educational systems in Western Europe are designed to help them achieve educational success. On the other hand, in Eastern Europe the education of the above-mentioned categories of students is also a goal of the local policies, which does not change the fact that more pressure is applied to assimilate them into a certain social and cultural system. The students should clearly fit into specific social roles, an idea which is rather absent in Western Europe, where celebrating diversity does not necessarily mean transforming the object contributing with its *otherness* to the diversity itself.

Therefore, the other and the concept of otherness in the educational sphere play an important part in constructing educational programs such as various student exchange projects or educational reforms postulated all over Europe, trying to include those who were once excluded from the system, e.g. diverse ethnic minorities. The educational concept of *otherness* is considered here as a key factor in changing the way we teach our children to move towards a better and more diverse system. No matter whether we think of *otherness* related to the migration processes or *otherness* related to regional differences within Europe, this category is a constant companion of the cultural shift we are experiencing at the moment. However, nowadays this idealistic approach seems to undergo a clear decrease due to certain events which have placed a significant question mark over the view of our own societies as pluralistic, modern and democratic units of a global community.

We may ask ourselves how anthropology and education differ in the way they tackle the same problem – the presence of the *other* in the cultural process shaping our worldviews. Is there any difference at all, or do anthropology and pedagogy take parallel paths, close to each other but still separate? This question emerged in the United States in the early 20th-century. A growing number of migrants from Europe and Asia, a yet unsolved problem of native Americans and the racial discourse related to Afro-Americans, contributed to the construction of a new approach towards studying educational phenomena in relation to culture. This new perspective emerged within American anthropological circles and was supposed to provide answers to the question of the changing American cultural identity. Scholars like Ruth Benedict, Margaret Mead, or the father of the American anthropology, Franz Boas (a German immigrant himself), undertook this mission with a profound assumption that cultural diversity is not a problem to overcome but a natural characteristic of culture itself. The cultural patterns of the Italian immigrants arriving in New York, the strange rituals of the American Indians or the social marginalization of the Afro-Americans had introduced important issues to solve, that is, to understand the manner in which the *other* thinks, and how to arrive at conclusions of how his worldviews affect his actions. These issues are even more important since the United States became an economic superpower and the American society has to invent a new educational system which could produce a new type of the American citizens – aware of their cultural and ethnic background but also able to identify with their national values and American culture. The anthropology of education in its American form reveals a very pragmatic approach, dealing with schooling systems, educational institutions, educational ideologies and the category of difference, visible in all the areas mentioned above.

In the second half of the 20th-century similar questions were also raised in Europe, along with the processes of decolonization and the post-war social dynamics of change affecting most western European societies. The *other* became not just visible in the streets of London or Paris, but it also demanded participation in the social and political life of the continent. Various emancipation groups, counterculture movements, alternative communities and youth subcultures have spread throughout Europe since the end of the 1950s. Anthropology and pedagogy have tried to grasp this dynamically changing cultural landscape using old theories and methods. Frequently, the question of the application of the traditional humanistic approach is raised in both of the aforementioned academic fields, pointing out its limitations. The need for a new view of culture and *otherness* emerged, leading to a dramatic change of the perspective in pedagogical and anthropological examinations of the adaptation processes in modern Europe. A growing social discontent has been reflected in the paradigm shift in the social sciences. The finger of cultural criticism was pointed towards hegemonic ideologies and groups being the former centers of power. The European culture changes and so does the educational discourse surrounding it. One can observe that critical pedagogy through the works of Paulo Freire or Henry Giroux has deconstructed the modernist order of things. It can also be witnessed how anthropology is moving from its field of interest, lying upon traditional and primitive communities, towards the modern culture of the western society. From now on the imperative of the interpretative understanding of the *other* is shared by both academic disciplines.

On the other hand, the cultural phenomena occurring in contemporary Europe may lead to the notion that this very open and pluralistic view of the cultural awareness is just an ideological façade and it is not shared by all Europeans themselves, but rather by their intellectual elites. The controversies surrounding the presence of the cultural *otherness* in the French educational and social context provide a significant example of how the category of difference is constructed and perceived in a society built upon the noble ideas of the Great Revolution and the Enlightenment. The eruption of street violence in the Paris suburbs a few years ago was the consequence of this differentiation.[7] The French media discourse related to these noble ideas was based on the argumentation provided by French citizens commenting on the events. They often expressed the view that violence was somehow a consequence of the undefined "natural" criminal characteristics of the youth and the people living on the outskirts of Paris full of drug dealers, thieves, people living only on welfare, and not ready and willing to take a decent job. Nicolas Sarkozy, who was holding the position of the minister of internal affairs, supported this thesis in his public speeches, demanding to act more aggressively against those who fight the police and disobey the authorities. The fact that the majority of the rioters had an immigrant background (mostly Algerian) was the key point in setting the distinction. Yet, although their parents and grandparents were born in Algeria and other Arabic countries, they were mostly born in France and had a full French citizenship. In their view they were symbolically deprived of their "Frenchness" by the state authorities (the police and politicians), who were supposed to grant them citizen's rights.

France is also torn apart by the discussion regarding the Muslim burkas and niqabs worn in public institutions such as schools. A central question raised here refers to the nature of these traditional clothes. Do burkas and niqabs symbolise one's belonging to the community of the faithful Muslims? If so, the division of religion and state symbols does not allow them to be worn in public institutions, especially by teachers who are state officials. But perhaps they are a symbol of one's belonging to the ethnic minority? In this case France, being a modern, democratic and pluralistic state, cannot deprive its citizens of the right to manifest their ethnic identity. This paradoxical situation and the problems of how to solve it make the whole issue even more problematic. Thus, the question of our *otherness* expression frequently penetrates both cultural and political categories. This discursive pendulum may be found not only in France but also in many other European countries.

Great Britain remains among those countries facing the above-mentioned problem. The British issues regarding *otherness* also tend to be situated around the problem of Muslim communities in the UK and their role in the radicalization of Islam. This problem became even more important after the context of 9/11. Some of the imams living in Britain, like Abu Hamza,

[7] See R. Canet, L. Pech, M. Stewart, "France's Burning Issue: Understanding the Urban Riots of November 2005," in forthcoming B. Bowden, M. David (eds.), *Riot: Resistance and Rebellion in Britain and France. 1381 to the Present*, 2013. Online version: http://papers.ssrn.com/sol3/papers.cfm?abstract_id=1303514 [date of entry: 12.12.2013].

called upon their followers to rise up against the British state and to replace it with some kind of Islamic religious caliphate.[8] Radical and dangerous as it may be, this postulate is only shared by the minority of British Muslims, which results in the fact that Abu Hamza and other radical imams are not supported by the British Muslim and Arab communities as a whole. Unfortunately, this does not change the fact that the demonization of Muslims in the UK is built upon this kind of events. Today, the British *other* is mostly associated with radical Islamists, some of whom were born and raised in the UK, marking the whole issue of national identity and providing a battlefield for the British National Party, a patriotic and racist *right wing* political group. Furthermore, similar anti-Muslim sentiments were visible during the recent London riots, where a small group of Muslim radicals distributed stickers proclaiming Sharia law in some London districts as a form of a specific self-defence model of the local community.

In modern Europe these and other examples of the construction and debates surrounding the issue of cultural *otherness* constitute the most important obstacle in implementing the ideas of the educational anthropology, which could be considered as a sub-discipline of both anthropology and pedagogy. Frequently, educational institutions and the current ideologies of teaching consider the cultural difference as a necessary part of the social reality. At the same time in the old-fashioned way they tend to set a strategy of cultural inclusion of the *other*. The anthropology of education conducted by modern researchers in Europe aims both to point out this paradox and to deconstruct the way *otherness* is treated within specific cultural discourses. The way we conceptualize the category of cultural difference today is still affected by our view of culture as a whole – as a system among other systems. This idea is also to be found in contemporary social, cultural and political discourses in European societies, which until now considered themselves as liberal and open toward *otherness*. Nowadays, a popular view of *otherness* as a threat to our own culture gains an increasing support in countries like Sweden and the Netherlands, where national sentiments have become an important part of the public discourse. In these countries educational systems are undergoing a deep change related to their ideological foundations. Facing the failure of the assimilation policy of the Dutch or Swedish schooling systems and yet remaining one of the most liberal in Europe, they

[8] http://www.dailymail.co.uk/news/article-2019547/Anjem-Choudary-Islamic-extremists-set-Sharia-law-zones-UK-cities.html [date of entry: 12.12.2013].

have reversed the policy of a soft cultural change to introduce a „harder" education of immigrants, especially when it comes to the matter of language competence. As illustrated by the recent debates in Germany over the rejection of the idea of the so-called "multi-kulti Gessellschaft" (multicultural society), this tendency marks a growing phenomenon in Europe.

Being a relatively new discipline, anthropology of education tries to capture particular cultural processes of change such as assimilation, acculturation or socialization in the context of the culture itself. Therefore, it brings into the discussion an attempt to understand the character of cultural shifts put against the background of the social praxis. The structural character of the aforementioned leap from idea into praxis helps us to grasp this particular problem in its essential form. In the European context, anthropology of education is applied towards the schooling of students who do not meet specific requirements. When facing problems such as a migrant background, physical handicap, or social exclusion, these obstacles could be overcome through the integration process. Anthropology of education shows how to apply this idea without implementing our own worldview into the minds of people who do not share our views. That is why anthropology of education may serve as an example of a discipline which, on the one hand, aims at contributing to a practical change in the cultural reality and its functions and, on the other hand, avoids the trap of the ideologization of the educational sphere.

Chapter 3

Culture does matter. The American "boarding schools" system and the transformations of the assimilative policy in the USA

Cultures are never static wholes. Moreover, their systemic character manifests those features that are the most characteristic and typical ones for a particular case more often than not in the process of change. The dynamics of these changes directly influences the particular constituents of a given culture, regardless of whether we speak here of institutions, values, symbols, or the very human individuals and their world views. A cultural change is reflected in human minds and orientates our own actions towards the uncertain future. It influences our adaptation abilities and stimulates the process of transforming our foregoing world views into a new set of ideas in terms of quality. Of course, the range of the process of cultural change always depends on the context in which it takes place. A change taking place in the context of a modern democratic political order will assume a different character from the one that accompanies the situation of a forcible clash between cultures, a conflict, or a war. Notwithstanding this, the problem of cultural change with regard to the interpenetration of cultural systems, as well as the decline of selected cultural content, or even whole cultural systems, constitutes an issue which has been a research topic frequently raised throughout the last few decades, both in the spheres of culture science (anthropology, sociology) and pedagogy. In this last case, the pedagogical debate on cultural change concerns the issues of the interpenetration of cultures within the field of education, as well as with regard to the ideology of teaching and the roles which schools and universities play in this process. Pedagogy often strives to indicate in this respect a range and direction of changes that affect those age groups who are the most susceptible to change and who also are the first to adapt (young people) to their environment, or who accept it in the most obstructive manner (older generations). The pedagogical debate concerning the adaptation of the representatives of one culture to some new conditions designated by a different cultural system in the sphere of institutional education also shows significant diversity, depending on the type of society in which this process takes place. Indeed, it is more active in countries where the issue of multiculturalism is an important problem, just as it is the case with the need for developing a strategy of dealing with the presence of people with a different culture in a system that strives to preserve its homogeneous identity.

Indeed, the problem of cultural adaptation in a situation of the emerging model of multicultural society has become included in the sphere of interests of researchers in those countries where a cultural reality of this type is a fact. Therefore, similar questions have been asked in the United States, Canada and Australia, more or less at the same time. In many respects, the answers too were similar, but they were also different in significant aspects, depending on a given country and its particular context. However, it was the researchers in the USA in particular who had been involved in the debate mentioned above, especially in the period when the American society underwent far-reaching transformations in terms of its cultural and ethnic face for the first time, i.e. at the turn of the 19th and the 20th-century. However, the American pedagogical theory and practice pursued at the turn of the centuries could not of course at that time have been compared with today's image of this branch of knowledge. At the time, the problem of internal cultural changes, a considerable surge of immigrants from Europe and Asia, as well as the quickly emerging ethnic minorities, or the slow emancipation of minorities of a social and cultural character (African Americans), involved mainly the problem of assimilating them into the culture of the white majority, which constituted the core of the American society, as soon as possible. The problem was and still is the very social and cultural substrate coming from the society of that time, which used to be called *W.A.S.P.* in the American nomenclature of the subject, which is an acronym for the term *White Anglo-Saxon Protestant*. It invokes the social current that identifies itself with the past and the tradition of the first English colonisers of North

America. Thus, not only has the issue of cultural assimilation been raised as a research topic, but it has also become an interpretation of educational practice in the United States with regard to those groups who did not belong to the predominant current.

This is precisely what occurred in the case of the indigenous peoples, who were one of the most marginalized minority groups in the USA until the first half of the 20th-century. Their marginalization consisted, first and foremost, in an actual, long-term social, economic and spatial isolation of American Indians, which translated into a further and deeper debarment of that group from the cultural *mainstream*. However, the process of marginalizing Indians in the American society was not initiated together with the first contacts between the white settlers and the indigenous inhabitants of the New World. Its most important stage took place in the second half of the 19th-century – in the age when the American society was gaining its modern 20th-century form. It was an age of a rapid development in America, in terms of both its economy and culture. However, this change required a national unification in the name of the positivist ideals of development. What seemingly hindered this development were people who embodied civilisation backwardness, savagery and an antithesis to anything the white Americans wanted to be in the forthcoming decades. American Indians, or rather their lifestyle and culture (in the form it assumed at the time), constituted a significant obstacle in building the future society of prosperity and increased consumption. The traditional Indian beliefs and rites (which were beyond the comprehension of many people), reluctance in adopting Christianity, clashes and conflicts with the settlers who were pressing ahead to the west of the continent, or outright hostility towards the state perceived as an alien creation made by the white invaders, were frequent arguments against allowing the Indians to maintain their foregoing lifestyles. The Indian culture was to be totally absorbed by the culture of the white majority and there was no margin of error within which selected items of that culture might have been preserved.

The process of cultural assimilation was to be a total process that would penetrate an individual, starting from the most rudimentary foundations of their identity, to the most general issues related to popularising specific moral models, dress code, or manners. The education of the indigenous youth according to the model outlined by the late-Victorian morality became the main task put forward by federal authorities and educational institutions. However, the education of Indians had to proceed not only according to the specified direction designated by general directives of the assimilation policy, but also it had to answer the still emerging obstacles related to the application of the school methodology of the time in specific cases of particular tribes. The use of unified methods of upbringing and educational curricula often proved to miss the point with regard to the very diverse cultural topography of the indigenous America. This process proceeded in a different manner in the case of Indians from the east coast, who had already been strongly assimilated since the end of the 17th-century, and it was all the more different in the case of tribes inhabiting the south-west part of today's United States (that is, such states as Arizona or New Mexico), who were the last to submit to the pressure of assimilation and accept the supremacy of the authorities in Washington towards the end of the 19th-century. The fact still remains, however, that in each of these cases the ideology of assimilation and the then-current policy implemented on its basis left deep marks on the indigenous communities that were directly affected by them. They have also contributed to the popularisation of a set of common, most often (yet not only) traumatic elements of the experience of many generations of indigenous Americans. They have remained a heavy burden on the conscience of contemporary American education up till the present day. It was that education within which the attempts to come to terms with the darker side of the history of this country have been made since the 1960s, including the past of the "boarding schools."

The model of schools intended for the indigenous peoples, developed towards the end of the 19th-century in the United States and most often assuming the form of residential schools with very strict discipline (according to both today's standards and the ones of the time) has become a determinant of the then-actual policy of cultural assimilation. What is interesting, the mechanism of assimilation used in the United States at that time applied to the same extent to indigenous Americans and to the people coming to the USA in great numbers in search of a better future, i.e. poor immigrants from Italy or Ireland, who were landing by the score on the landing pier in New York, and then quickly inhabited the ethnic ghettos in the city. Those people, owing to the use of an assimilation model, were supposed to be quickly absorbed by the American society. Their tradition, language and ethnic identity were supposed to blur into an ocean of other ones, thus forming a common cultural front of America.

However, speaking of cultural assimilation in this case, it is required to take it into consideration of the ambiguous nature of the very concept with regard to the processes taking place within the American society at that time. The assimilation of Indians proceeded in a slightly different manner that was the case with newcomers from Europe, who were much closer to the Americans in terms of their culture. Sometimes, cultural assimilation was used to name a process of learning English by the immigrants, and another time to name the process of learning American values through citizenship education. In the case of Indians, assimilation referred to the process of a total and compulsory rooting out all that connected that group to their old lifestyle – from their language to their dress code. As a result, the indigenous Americans who completed their courses in schools intended especially for them were only to constitute another one among the elements which the mosaic of the American ethnic melting pot consists of. Their own identity was intended to melt down into an ocean of the remaining identities; they were not valued in any way, provided that they did not diverge too much from the model outlined by W.A.S.P. Otherwise, such an identity, expressing its otherness in public and marking the presence of this category in the official discourse, threatened the integrity of the American state and society by introducing the argument of multiculturalism to the debate – an argument that could not yet be granted the possibility of being articulated in the second half of the 19th-century. It occurred only after several decades, along with the changes which affected America in the 20th-century. That was the time when a significant change in the assimilation policy towards indigenous people, as well as in the strategy of conducting boarding schools, became noticeable.

At that time, the cultural assimilation of American Indians, put into practice to the greatest extent through education, was a phenomenon that was treated as the natural order of things and, at the same time, as a top-down social experiment. On the one hand, its inevitability was being pointed out, but on the other, the merits of the white teachers in "civilizing" the Indians were emphasised. This dialectic character of the assimilation process of the time derives its conceptual base from earlier ideological figures, formed as early as in 17th-century, when America was the New World; a country where the English Puritans could pursue their vision without fear – the vision of a society built completely from scratch and according to Christian values untainted (just as the Indians) by the Catholic tradition.

The religious character of the first attempts to educate the Indians also left its clear mark on the classic, 19th-century residential schools. It was also at that time, as it had been the case in the 17th-century, that the education process was perceived in terms of a continuation of the evangelism mission.

It was presented as a perpetual fight for the souls of the Indians, as well as for their status as rightful human beings and American citizens. However, the 17th-century base for that educational system has proved to be an important factor in the shaping of its later operation, including the contemporary dimensions of the operation of these schools in the USA, thus being a direct forbearer of the boarding schools of the turn of the 19th and 20th-century. In this context, maintaining ideological continuity concerns both the process of transforming the American education and the assimilation policy equally.

The first American schools and universities where the education curriculum for Indians was implemented had an openly inclusivist character. This was because a peaceful coexistence of white settlers and the local people was in the interest of both parties. Even the famous Harvard University had an appropriate institution that educated Native Americans for some time. However, this image is not strictly as ideal as it might seem. European colonisers strove to influence the indigenous communities with the ideals of Protestant proselytism from the very beginning of their presence on the American continent. Teaching Native Americans in accordance with the Protestant interpretation of the Holy Scripture was the most frequent way of incorporating them into the mainstream of public life. Mission schools were brought into existence mainly in the New England area. It was also there that the religious model could be noticed in its strongest form. Over time, the evangelisation of the Indians became "a public motive with a long history" in the United States.[1]

The process of educating Native Americans was symbolically initiated in 1612 by Pastor Alexander Whitaker in Jamestown, Virginia, when he undertook to educate an Indian girl called Pocahontas.[2] He renamed her with a Christian name Rebecca and sent her on a journey to England, so that she would acquire competencies purportedly natural for a white man. This case became a metaphorical representation and a certain canon of the further process of assimilating the indigenous people in America. Education was supposed to be carried out not so much owing to the fact of making Indians acquainted with the cultural attainments of the Europeans and the Protestant theological theses, but more through life experience – by making the indigenous people plunge into the way of life of the white newcomers. This was reflected in the words of one of the Protestant Evangelists of the

[1] R. W. Cogley, *John Eliot's mission before King Philip's War*, Harvard 1999, p. 2.

[2] H. G. Unger (ed.), *Encyclopedia of American Education*, New York 2007, p. 66.

time, John White, who said in 1630 that: "»the example of our course of living« would by God's blessing... make way for religion."[3]

Many other religious leaders of those years followed in Pastor Whitaker's footsteps, including Pastor Thomas Mayhew or Pastor John Eliot. The latter significantly contributed to the quickening of the crystallisation of the assimilation policy towards the Indians in the 17th-century. Eliot, a Protestant theologian and teacher of merit, saw a broader goal in the education of Indians from the very beginning of his activity, namely, the development of a new model for the American society. That model was intended to be a novelty in terms of its quality and become a trigger for a deep reform of Western values and a change of the religious paradigm. Seen from this perspective, America became a battlefield where the fight for the future American society, independent of England and Europe and pursuing its own pattern of existence, broke out. To a certain extent, it provides an explanation for the affective character of the education policy promoted by Eliot and other thinkers akin to him. On the other hand, the emotional attitude towards pursuing the goal set themselves by the Protestant teachers resulted from theological disputations carried on at that time on the issue of whether the Indians were human beings and whether they had souls.[4]

A religious interpretation of the motivations that stand behind the education of the Indians gains new significance in view of the actions undertaken in English colonies in the New World during that period. England, while fighting against the Catholic powers in the Old Continent, was looking for a new foothold and an opportunity to reinforce their own political and military potential. The assimilation of the Indians performed in accordance with London's targets could have significantly contributed to the change of the balance of power in Europe, caught up in religious wars.[5] Thus, they spared no expense to make the implementation of this idea possible. In 1649, the English Parliament brought the *Company for the Propagation of the Gospel in New England* into existence. Its task was, first of all, to acquire financial means in Europe, which were intended to support the actions undertaken by Mayhew and Eliot in America. Owing to gaining the support needed, Eliot

[3] R. W. Cogley, *John Eliot's mission before King Philip's War*, Harvard 1999, p. 5.

[4] At this point, it is required to recall the disputation which has been carried out since the end of the 16th-century by European theologians with regard to the colonisation of Central and Southern America.

[5] Let us remember that at the same time the dispute over supremacy in the New World was being conducted simultaneously by England, France and Spain.

was able to purchase two thousand acres of land near Boston in 1651, where he established the first school primarily intended for educating the Indians. That institution, initially known as the *Eliot School*, gained the reputation of being one of the best education facilities of such a profile quite quickly.[6]

However, the Pastor's plan reached much further. He intended to create not only a network of Indian schools, but also the whole social environment that would constitute the base for a new community. These actions resulted in bringing local Indian communities into existence – i.e. the so-called "praying Indians" and gathered small cities that were carefully planned in terms of space ("praying towns"). These cities attracted a large number of Indian converts, although it is required to remember that the motivations standing behind joining these communities were often significantly different from what their creators had intended.[7] Until 1675, Eliot and Mayhew managed to convert approx. 2.5 thousand Indians to Christianity, which constituted approx. 20% of the whole indigenous population in New England at that time.

The educational and assimilative success of Eliot allowed the model of education he developed to be popularised in other areas of North America, including the territory of today's Canada. Moreover, he wanted to establish close relations between Indian cultures and the white settlers, so that the Indians would be able to understand the world view of the settlers. He was one of the first to have translated the Holy Scripture into one of the languages belonging to the Algonquin group. He also published many other texts on the problem of educating these communities. One of them is the text titled "The Logic Primer" published in 1672. It offers an interpretation of the main rules of Protestantism, as well as a reflection of the assimilative ideology shared by Eliot himself and many other figures of the evangelical movement in America at that time. Its basic rules were based on the assumption of the existence of a deep difference in the world view presented by the Europeans and the indigenous peoples. In order to overcome this, it was required to undertake gradual educational and mission actions, resulting in the deep cultural assimilation of the Indians.[8] The four-stage assimilation plan was to

[6] What is interesting is the fact that the facility mentioned above still exists and is known as the *Eliot School of Fine and Applied Arts.*

[7] The undertow of motives for religious conversion was often the economic and political situation of groups of Indians at that time, who were decimated by endemic diseases brought to them by the white colonisers and there was not much room left for them, thus forcing them to make inconvenient alliances with the white people.

[8] See R. W. Cogley, *John Eliot's mission before King Philip's War*, Harvard 1999.

be started from teaching the most fundamental points for the people of that age – the way of life of the Europeans. Learning the 17th-century canon of behaviour included education in the sphere of social order (law), European technologies (crafts and farming) and the ruling manners (customs).

Once these obstacles had been removed, i.e. the dimensions of life indicated here had been inculcated into the Indians, they were ready for the second step, i.e. the acceptance of Christian teaching in the manner of Protestantism. However, in order to achieve this, it was required to get rid of all remnants of traditional beliefs. The religiousness of the Indians, referred to as devil worship, idolatry or image worship by the missionaries, had to give way to Christianity. Thus, religious education meant a process of full integration into the new faith, in the sphere of both the understanding of religious content and basic theological issues, and the knowledge of Protestant rituals. What is interesting, the white settlers equated the process of religious education with the civilization process at that stage. Both spheres, religion and civilization, were purportedly intended for complementing each other and to be mutually dependent. Thus, social order was to result from the divine order present in human souls. At the moment of accepting this fact, the Indians were willing to go to the third stage of assimilation, i.e. religious conversion proper. It was not before they had become Christians that the Indians were able to finish this process through active participation in social life, which constituted the fourth and last stage of changing their cultural identity.

Over time, however, this 17th-century educational and assimilative template started to submit to a slow degeneration. The ideals promoted by Eliot or Mayhew began to blur, clashing with the (actual) practice of treating the indigenous Americans in the years to come. The pragmatism of the new settlers pressing ahead to the west of the continent and forcing the Indians out of their former lands did not provide for putting an effort into the educational undertakings that could slightly mitigate the moment of contact. Taking as much land as possible before others did the same became the imperative for the action of the settlers. However, there was also a breakthrough when the United States gained independence, which had been preceded by debates carried out by the subsequent leaders of the nation. George Washington, Thomas Jefferson and Henry Knox determined the most important directions in the debates in this respect. Notwithstanding this, nevertheless, their considerations on the future lot of the indigenous peoples within the independent American state were also based on the

Protestant experience that had originated a hundred years previously. During the American Revolution, the *Committee on Indian Affairs* was established and one of its tasks was to refer "a minister of the gospel, to reside among the Delewere Indians, and isntruct them in the Christian religion; a schoolmaster to teach their youth reading, writing, and arithmetic."[9]

Washington and Knox clearly specified the direction of the future assimilation policy, as well as the need for creating appropriate institutions that would work exclusively on the education of the Indians. That need was to constitute a significant supplementation of the policy. The indigenous Americans had to become useful for the American society. Otherwise, there was no need for including them in the public life and allowing them to pursue self-realization outside the areas specified as future reservations. Thus, learning the crafts was promoted among the Indians, appropriate amounts were allocated for this purpose and experienced craft guild masters were sent to the areas occupied by hospitable Indian communities. This policy bore fruit in the emergence of a group of white people who called themselves "friends of the Indians" and who operated as mediators between the government and indigenous communities. From now on, the religious mission was replaced with a civilization mission, although the religious aspect of educating the Indians was graphically evident for a long time. For instance, the Presbyterian representatives of the *American Board of Commissioners for Foreign Missions* had assigned considerable financial means for the establishment of Indian schools in the states of New York, Vermont, Tennessee and Mississippi as early as in the beginning of the 19th-century. At the turn of the 18th and 19th-century, however, the education of Indians assumed the shape that was to set the limits of educating all these groups within the American society, which diverged from the established white Protestant canon in terms of culture, for the forthcoming decades. That system became expressed in full in the second half of the 19th-century and determined the educational experience of many Americans of indigenous origin until the 1920s. However, what contributed to the change of attitude of the white majority towards the Indians in the field of education was the change of the nature of institutional relations. Insofar as these relations were not formalised to a large extent in the 17th-century, from the beginning of the 19th-century they became based on treaties concluded between

[9] Quote after: C. E. Trafzer, J. A Keller, L. Sisquoc, "Origins and Development of the Indian Boarding School System," in C. E. Trafzer, J. A Keller, L. Sisquoc (eds.), *Boarding School Blues. Revisiting American Indian Educational Experiences*, Nebraska 2006, p. 8.

the government in Washington and the particular tribes that inhabited the area of the United States. At that time, land property relations also changed significantly, especially after passing the *Indian Removal Act* in 1830, which forced the majority of Indians from the east coast of the USA to move to the west of the Mississippi.

It is startling, however, that the system of classic Indian schools (*boarding schools*) was relatively short-lived, for it lasted only throughout two decades between 1879 and 1902. The vast majority of these facilities were modelled after the first Indian school, the *Carlisle Indian Industrial School*, established in 1879 and created by Richard Henry Pratt, a former officer of the army of the USA. This school implemented a curriculum based on an educational experiment which Pratt had undertaken just after the end of the American Civil War. It consisted in an attempt to educate a group of prisoners of Indian origin and teaching them the basic social competencies. The words of the founder himself became the credo of the school. He defined his educational goal in the following manner: "The Indian is a man like other men. He has no innate or inherent qualities that condemn him to separation from other men or generations of slow development." Therefore: "to civilize the Indian place him in the midst of civilization; to keep him civilized make him stay."[10]

Pratt's idea for educating the Indians was highly commended across the United States, quickly inscribing itself into the policy of the government towards indigenous groups which was conducted at that time. Towards the end of the 19th-century, it was supposedly based on a specific combination of positivist ideology and the popular understanding of the rules of social evolutionism. Seen from this perspective, the assimilation of Indians was both a political task and a scientific experiment at the same time. However, its outcome, i.e. the symbolic transformation of Indians into white people, was uncertain. Thus, it was required to intensify the educational actions aimed at ensuring the success of the whole undertaking. The school strictness used in the Indian schools, which has been mentioned before, fuelled controversy even at the time when these schools operated in their shape in question. The use of direct coercion and other forms of physical and symbolic violence were the order of the day in these institutions.[11] It

[10] Quote after: J. Fear-Segal, "Nineteenth-Century Indian Education: Universalism Versus Evolutionism," *Journal of American Studies*, 33/1999, p. 330.

[11] For instance, students who dared to use their native language instead of English in school or in the dormitory had their mouths washed with soap.

is also required to remember that hard, manual labour was an important element of the upbringing in these institutions. It purportedly contributed to a peculiar ennoblement of the Indians, who were "lazy by nature" (this was how they were stereotypically perceived at that time). Schools based on the model from Carlisle started to be created across the whole area of the USA, introducing only slight modifications to the original concept. The most important of them include such facilities as, e.g.: *Chemawa Indian School* in Salem, Oregon, *Chilocco Indian Agricultural School* in Chilocco, Oklahoma, *Haskell Indian Industrial Training School* in Lawrence, Texas, or *Sherman Indian High School* in Riverside, California. A total of approx. 60 facilities of this type were created during the mentioned period.

Along with the beginning of the 20th-century, however, some significant changes, both in the system of educating the indigenous peoples and in the assimilation policy (albeit to a lesser extent), could be observed. The so-called Meriam Report, published in 1928, which elucidated abnormalities and malpractices in these schools, contributed to a slight transformation in their operation. However, the proper breakthrough occurred in the second half of the 20th-century. Along with the emancipation of minority groups in the USA, such as African Americans or Latin Americans, the American Indians also gained a clear voice in the debate on the possibilities of cultural and political self-determination. Owing to the activity of such initiatives as the *American Indian Movement*, for instance, it has been possible to develop a new educational model. Those of the Indian schools which had not been closed, were transformed into high schools with a curriculum profile which does not diverge considerably from the majority of schools in the United States. The unification of education was timed to coincide with the change of the assimilation policy in America. Many factors influenced this state of affairs, e.g. the emergence of the so-called ethnics – people who share the type of a hybrid identity which combines the pan-American identity with their identification with minority groups into a coherent whole. Furthermore, population transformations in the USA, which we have been able to observe for several decades, have also forced a redefinition of the relations between the federal government, the indigenous peoples and the immigrant groups.

The process of transformation of both levels in question, the educational one and the political one, went collaterally to a large extent. For many years, the education of Indians in the United States has formed part of a specified cultural and political ideology pursued with a lot of enthusiasm until recently, by both government institutions and non-governmental units, as well as by people who perceive the process of "civilising" the Indians as a quasi-religious goal of their own lives. Notwithstanding this, the phenomenon of Indian schools remains one of the most important aspects of the structuring of the American variant form of the debate on multiculturalism. At present, it co-creates the debate which has become increasingly visible in the conceptualisation of the American identity and the concept of national community. The present activity of schools that are successors of the Indian schools shows that it is possible to create an educational curriculum that reconciles the requirements of the modern times with the elements of the cultural tradition of indigenous Americans, discovered anew and invigorated by the students.

Chapter 4

Multiculturalism reconsidered. Bilingual education in Guatemala

We may fairly say that over five hundred years after the arrival of Europeans in the New World most of the Latin American societies did change significantly in terms of their social structure and national culture. Just recently, we had witnessed a widespread emergence of various emancipatory movements across the Americas which happened in the last two decades; each of them attracting the indigenous population into the mainstream on a different scale. This process has clearly drawn attention onto the field of politics and culture in countries like Bolivia or Mexico, who face a similar problem. This problem is caused by the co-existence of two cultural streams, the followers of which not necessarily share the same interests, values and culture, In consequence of the existing gap between these two, the attempts at reconciliation and dialogue are still considered by many as destined to fail. The first of the mentioned streams connects the white and mestizo culture in a broad sense of a Western and European tradition.[1] It is based on an assumption that there might be just one direction of social modernization i.e. accepting the dominant role of the Western civilization. The other one, however, joins diverse native groups, who often differ culturally from each other to a large extent and until now did not build a consistent

[1] In relation to the context of Central and South America, the use of the term *mestizo* is the most accurate. It describes a general process of race mixing (*mestizaje*), as well in cultural terms (*mestizaje cultural*). It is also very risky to use the term *Creole* in this context as in most Latin American countries (except the Caribbean region) it is associated clearly with the descendants of Spanish colonizers.

front of indigenous organizations. The reality of the last years has shown that this doesn't have to be the case and more and more native Americans are promoting a vision of a pan-American movement for indigenous rights. Culture and politics have become thus in the last decades an issue of high importance throughout the whole Latin American region after long years of conflict. To understand the nature of the conflict we have to acknowledge the fact that the confrontation of the two worlds mentioned above has existed since the first contact of Europeans with the native populations, marked by violence, injustice and suffering, and which still is imprinted in this manner in the collective social memory. The Indio was for a long period of time a figure of instrumentalized politics against anyone who does not accept the dominance of white culture and identifies himself with the indigenous tradition. Cultural assimilation and acculturation were taken for granted as a tool of modernization. The clash between the proposed western future and the indigenous past has divided the Latin American societies into a dichotomy of modern white societies and marginalized rural Indios, whose cultural and political activism was for a long period of time considered as insignificant in terms of national culture.

Today the cultural and political sphere is, however, still troublesome in the Latin American context, as it tackles the issue of the historical relations of Native Americans and the descendants of European conquerors. The historical aspect of those relations affects contemporary discourse on Latin American societies on a wide scale. This specific merging of past and present might be regarded here, as well as the constant element of the Latin American reality. Especially when it comes to the indigenous aspect of the phenomenon, the aforementioned duality seems to direct the societies of the region into a complex discussion on their future. As the celebrated Mexican author and Cervantes Prize winner, Carlos Fuentes states in relation to the situation in his home country: "The Indian world of Mexico offers an opposition between the visible and the invisible. [...] The European conquest of Mexico left the Indians a defeated people, and sometimes a defeated people prefer to go unnoticed. They become at one with darkness, wishing to be forgotten so as not to be struck once more. [...] The Indians became a part of the Terra Incognita."[2]

A significant change began along with the processes of national reconciliation, including peace talks between Latin American governments

[2] C. Fuentes, *A New Time for Mexico*, Berkeley and Los Angeles 1997, pp. 27–28.

and left- and rightwing paramilitary organizations. Slowly the societies of the region started to accept the ongoing change as a necessary aspect of modernization in a global context. The division between the white and mestizo elites and indigenous groups also started to crumble. More and more native organizations, intellectuals and activists joined the efforts to overcome the existing obstacles and participated in the social, political and economic reforms in states like Mexico, Colombia or Brazil. The movement towards a better, more democratic future has been made thanks to many initiatives undertaken not just by mainstream personas, but also by indigenous organizations and people with no earlier political experience whatsoever.[3] Although the declarative side of this process became visible in the social debates, the social praxis has shown that the existing gap between these two factions is much deeper and harder to deal with than one could have thought. Historical animosities and existing stereotypes regarding both groups have once again shown their vitality. Cultural aspects of the planned social, political and economic reforms became an important point in plans for future prosperity. Countries with a large number of indigenous peoples, like for example Guatemala, were thus forced to deal with culture in the first place and a new approach towards the understanding of the term "national culture" had to be worked out.

The Central American state of Guatemala had also undergone in the early 1990's such a radical make-over when it comes to its political, social and cultural issues. This transgression was also typical for many other countries in Central and South America at that time. The ongoing peace process between leftist guerrillas and the government and right wing paramilitary militias, or the process of national reconciliation and dialogue, were significant for the contemporary shape of the Guatemalan society. However, the specific structure of that society is being still characterized by an existing conflict between two main groups – the descendants of the Spanish conquistadores and mestizos on one side (so called ladinos) and the native Indios on the other that is all the groups identifying themselves with the indigenous population and culture. The gap is being made here (just like in similar cases in Mexico or Bolivia) by a long lasting historical discrepancy between the ladinos being in power and the marginalized Indios. The conquest of the

[3] Many indigenous forms of political activism had at the beginning a very local character, and they were dealing with issues such as land partition and forms of labour division consistent with indigenous traditions. This is why land reforms are often a starting point and a central issue in all modernization debates in Latin America today.

Americas is therefore building an ideological discourse behind the social, cultural, economic and political diversification in today's Guatemala. As for a rural country with almost no natural resources, Guatemala is dependant on agriculture. Rural areas are inhabited mostly by the indigenous population, whose economic situation is dependant on land owners (latifundistas), mostly Spanish speaking ladinos, who hold 90% of the agricultural valuable land. Despite their large number in the national population statistics, poor, uneducated and mostly inhabiting rural areas Indios were in this context marginalized for a long period of time, pushed outside of the political and social mainstream, whose ideological basis was for the last few decades based on the rejection of indigenous culture and languages, seen by whites and mestizos as not worthy of any interest. This diversification of national culture in Guatemala was characteristic not just for this country, but also for the whole of Latin America. Native Americans were, and still are, perceived by a large part of the white societies as somehow inferior in terms of race and culture to the civilization of whites.

The contemporary linguistic landscape of Guatemala presents a very diverse picture. This diversification is related to a distinction based more on the difference of local languages belonging to the Mayan language family than a difference between various language families. This doesn't change the fact that the official language of Guatemala is still just the Spanish castellano. This situation is grounded in the constitutional act from 1965 called "Ley Orgánica de Educación," a legal act confirming the primary role of Spanish and the linguistic education as a part of the process of social development. Spanish was supposed to be in the eyes of the law makers a national language and the indigenous communities were supposed to be incorporated into the state system through advancing linguistic education. However, it doesn't mean that Spanish is broadly used by the Indio population today. Most of the Indio groups in Guatemala do not use this language on an everyday basis and it is not seldom that some Mayas don't speak Spanish at all. They use just the local Maya language related to the region they live in, a local community, or sometimes even to a particular township. The general number of contemporary Maya languages is being estimated as 51, including the local dialectal forms. Not so long ago two Mayan languages were functional, which today are being treated as extinct; however, the groups that used them remain as culturally separate groups. From this 51 we may distinguish 21 languages which belong to the Mayan linguistic family and this number makes up also the basic distinction of the country's ethnic diversification of the Mayan groups. These languages are: Acateko, Avalateco, Chuj, Chorti, Itzaj, Ixil, Kanjolobal, Q'aqchikel, Q'eqchi, Quiche, Mam, Mopan, Popti (Jakalteqo), Poqomchi, Poqomam, Sakapulteqo, Sipaqapense, Teko, Tzutijil, Uspanteko. This diversification appears more clearly when we accept the fact that 70% of all languages used in Guatemala are being more or less derived from just four of these Mayan languages – Quiche, Mam, Q'aqchikel and Q'eqchi. The last 30% is however divided into 16 various idioms.

Except for the Spanish and Maya languages, today in Guatemala are also being used languages with absolutely no linguistic relation to any of the Maya languages whatsoever. These are: the Garifuna language from the arawak family, and the isolated and treated as extinct Xinka language. The Garifuna language is being used by around 17 thousand people called the Black Caribs, which make up an ethnic group living on the Atlantic coast throughout Central America – starting from Belize and ending in Nicaragua. Its ethnic origins reach back to the end of the 17th-century, when the escaped black slaves mixed with native Caribs on the island of St. Vincent. After a military conflict with the British troops they changed their habitat to the coast of Honduras and spread slowly throughout the whole region. The Garifuna came to Guatemala by the end of the 18th-century as forced settlers and live today around the cities of Puerto Barrios and Livingston on the north east coast of the country. Contrary to the Garifuna, the Xinka language is not in use today and is considered as isolated, but a few researchers link it to the Lenca language. The Xinka ethnic group is still living in eight towns (municipios) in the department of Santa Rosa and uses Spanish.[4]

Mayan languages in Guatemala are being distinguished by a significant disproportion of the number of their users, ranging from small groups, counting a dozen elders (like in the case of Itzaj Maya) up to large groups counting almost 2 million people (like in the case of Quiche Maya). These discrepancies in the language structure have their consequences in the spatial placement and density of the population by the particular Maya groups. For example, the Q'eqchi Maya are dispersed over a vast area in the middle of Guatemala, but a comparatively large group of Q'aqchikel Maya inhabits a relatively small piece of land around the Atitlan Lake. Therefore, a precise description of the linguistic structure of the Maya groups may cause some difficulties. This situation has been caused by long lasting migrations of the

[4] L. Tzian, *Mayas y ladinos en cifras. El caso Guatemala*, Guatemala 1994, p. 25.

Maya population inspired by severe political repressions starting from the 1950's where the civil war broke out between the state and the guerillas. Migrations of whole Maya groups into areas far from their original homeland complicate every attempt to reconstruct the map of the genuine placement of all the Maya communities. Nonetheless, the most numerous groups of Maya dominate the landscape. The statistical relation of all the users of Maya languages, which we are able to identify with the category of Indio to the ladino population, is from 1 million 700 thousand to 3 million 800 thousand.

The proportions of the particular linguistic groups in Guatemala are also based on various statistics made by institutions and organizations which follow different political interests. These organizations don't have to always have a political character. The recent activism of religious denominations converting whole local communities may also affect the reliability of the sources.[5] Such an uncertain source of data is characteristic for the Guatemalan situation, not just in relation to languages. The political dimension is also attributed to many government and Maya initiatives in the field of linguistic education. The idea that a common national language is to be introduced is one of the basic tasks the Guatemalan state puts as a priority today. The practical realization of the unification of the society on the level of language is, however, put under a question mark. The attachment of the Maya people to their local languages is, in the eyes of the government, the main obstacle for achieving this goal. Governmental attempts directed towards homogenization of national culture (also through mono-linguistic politics) stand in a clear contradiction to the ideas of the Maya revitalization movements, which started to gain wide interest in the 1990's along with the peace process and the peace treaty signed in 1994. Therefore, the idea of cultural pluralism stands in opposition to the actions undertaken towards creating a single cultural pattern by the ladino elites. The consequence of this ideological clash is an inflammation of the existing animosities between the two groups. How the linguistic element of that conflict is being used by both sides becomes more clear when we include the fact that the Mayan

[5] One of the most known Protestant denominations interested in language politics and gathering data is the US based Summer Institute of Linguistics (SIL). The conversions from Catholicism (or folk version of the religion) to Protestantism were the most common in the last decades. There are also other non-Christian groups today active in Guatemala. There are reported cases of conversions to Islam of local traditional Maya communities. These are, however, related to the traditional political role of the village chief and his influence on other members of local communities.

languages today are an object of unification, for example through creating a unified alphabet, which is more adequate in the inscription of most of the Mayan languages. Such an alphabet was created already in 1991 and gained some popularity even among Maya groups in south Mexico. By that time the Mayan languages could formerly be inscribed correctly in the Latin alphabet only in a limited manner.

Nevertheless, the most effort in the process of the revitalization of Mayan culture in Guatemala is put into language education. Until the 1980's Spanish was the only language taught in public schools. Bilingual education started by the end of the decade and even then it was put into practice just in several isolated cases. Spanish lessons were for a long time an important part of the ladinization policy, which by the Guatemalan state was called castellinization. The breaking point for the language education of the Mayas was 1965. In that year a program called Castellinization Bilingue was launched with support from the United Nations. The program was dedicated to improving the methods of teaching Spanish to Mayan children and simultaneously to their inclusion into national culture by making it possible for the Indios to fulfill their educational duty. The employment of bilingual teachers made it possible for Mayan children to get closer to the civic model promoted by the state. Castellinzation Bilingue was functional until the 1970's, when the fight with the guerillas had escalated. The intensity of the fighting with leftist groups in the 1980's had contributed to the emergence of a situation where language policy has been merged with military violence and intense assimilation of the Indios, which had led to a decrease of the number of Mayas learning in public schools. An exception here is made by an initiative called Proyecto Nacional de Educacion Bilingue. The project started in 1981 and ended in 1984. Maya children, who graduated in a basic Spanish course in elementary schools still had limited competencies in using that language. The ministry of education had proposed teaching the children Spanish for two years, until they achieved a sufficient level. The program, financed one third by the American Agency for International Development had been welcomed by many ladinos hoping for a appeasement of the existing conflict which in their opinion had mostly a cultural basis. Even a new name for the first year of classes had been introduced (preprimaria instead of castellization) to diminish the image that the program's only goal was cultural assimilation. The project's demise had not changed much the educational situation of the Mayas. The Maya languages and culture were an object of ongoing assimilation efforts, and everything that had to do with them was to be eradicated (for example Maya languages with over a million users were deliberately called "dialects"). This official policy was not verymuch effective because of the fact that there were not enough schools and the enforcement of the educational duty had little effect. Of course, it also doesn't mean that Spanish was perceived by Mayas in that time just as a language of oppression. It was used widely as a communication tool on the level of ladino/indio relations and slowly also between various ethnic Maya groups. With time bilingual competencies became "a pragmatic solution to the enforcement of political and socio-economical powers."[6]

The knowledge of Spanish declared openly by many Mayas is therefore not a simple rejection of traditional cultural values. Many meetings of Maya organizations and institutions are being held in Spanish, which connects the members of these organizations on an interpersonal level. A good example of that mechanism is delivered by a Mayan Noble Peace Prize winner and Maya activist, Rigoberta Menchu Tum, who admitted that she had learned Spanish because of the need to communicate with activists from other Maya groups and to attract international attention to her cause. It is also a mistake if we assume that contemporary Mayas omit to learn other languages than their own. Often we may meet people who speak a handful of languages, including Spanish. However, we cannot say the same about the ladinos. The ladino are mostly reluctant when it comes to learning local Maya languages, as Spanish is still seen as the only national language by many of the people in big cities. An exception here is being made in the region of Alta Verapaz, where some German migrants settled and adopted the Q'eqchi language as their own.

It is quite clear that the issue of language education in today's Guatemala is not characterized by stagnation. Ley Organica de Educacion allowed the use of Maya languages in learning Spanish as a basis for further education. Today, plans are being made to introduce a new project called Programa Nacional de Educacion Bilingue (PRONEBI), which is supposed to change the language situation of the Mayas. Although the first outline of the project appeared already in 1984, it is the reality of the recent years which has made it into a praxis. It is being considered as an important tool in the Maya revitalization movement and in maintaining their cultural identity within the model of a future multicultural state. According to the

[6] R. McKenna-Brown, "The Mayan Language Loyalty Movement in Guatemala," in E. F. Fischer, R. McKenna-Brown (ed.), *Maya Cultural Activism in Guatemala*, Austin 1996, p. 167.

idea of the project, a common bilingual education in public schools is being planed – in Spanish and local Maya languages. The authors of the initiative call it "parallelism," in the sense that both languages should be developed equally. The idea has also been criticized by some ladinos, insisting that this project is being undertaken only by Indios for Indios. It doesn't change the fact that PRONEBI is troubled today by a lack of funds and is not on a level its authors would like to see it.

The lack of significant funding of bilingual education in Guatemala might be strange if we take into account that the former minister of education, Alfredo Tay Coyoy, was representing the Mayas as the first Indio official in the government. Nonetheless, the actions undertaken by Coyoy and other politicians has contributed to a new image of the Mayan struggle for self-determination. Education is today one of the most significant fields, where Mayan identity is being reframed. The cultural, social, political and economic transition affects the Maya in Guatemala in the same manner as other indigenous groups in Central and South America. This widespread phenomenon of revitalization and reconstruction of traditional cultures has an influence on the construction of pan-Indian networks throughout Latin America and even the United States and Canada. Language education is an integral part of the actions of many indigenous activists, and the situation in Guatemala may serve as a role model for societies of similar structure. Guatemalan educational initiatives are based on ideological foundations, which take the cultural basis for granted and try to popularize it among all Maya groups in the name of the pan-Mayan movement. Education is here taken as a sphere of articulation of such postulates for many Mayan activists and the new schooling institutions have a significant political role to fulfil. Recently created schools called escuelas de autogestion are being controlled by local communities, but they are also building a close working network of educational institutions across the country. These Escuelas Mayas take it as their goal to "incorporate education into the Mayan culture, and not to incorporate Mayan culture into schooling."[7] The politics of schooling in contemporary Guatemala is a part of a general effort to popularize cooperation among various Maya groups and to legitimize Mayan culture as an integral part of national cultural discourse. The so called "movement of linguistic loyalty" expresses those actions focused on strengthening the

---

[7] E. F. Fischer, R. McKenna-Brown (ed.), *Maya Cultural Activism in Guatemala*, Austin 1996, p. 220.

Maya identity and the process of reconciliation between the Indios and ladinos. This situation is recently taking shape in the educational field too, where bilingualism is more and more often seen as a necessary competence in building the future multicultural society.

The Guatemalan concept of multiculturalism is certainly a specific version of the idea of cultural and political pluralism, closely linked to the modernization of the country. The political ties between local Maya communities and ethnic groups are being perceived today as a beginning of the construction of a network of cooperation not just between the Mayas themselves, but also of all the indigenous people in Latin America, or even all former Third World countries. This movement is being perceived by many activists as a chance and an opportunity for bringing the postulates of the groups neglected until now by history into the light of world community attention. They are often joining forces with organizations and institutions which although they do not represent indigenous groups directly, still retain a similar worldview and political goals. A unified front of the Maya and other Indio groups and the alter- or anti-globalism movement became a significant power in shaping the social, economic and political processes in today's Latin America. The "turn left" in the politics of the region in the last years might be regarded here as a clear sign of progressive democratization in countries like Mexico or Guatemala. Certainly, democratic representation of ethnic minorities in these countries is still a question of future actions, but contemporary initiatives lead the way to doing so.

Nevertheless, they are being placed into the complex reality of the region. The postcolonial context of such actions like the language education projects in Guatemala is by the native groups of Mexico, Guatemala, or Bolivia perceived as a historical chance for a public expression of the Indio identity on a global scale. The engagement of Maya activists, language teachers and intellectuals is a factor of change contributing to the global dynamics of cultural and political transgressions, at least in relation to former postcolonial countries. They desperately need a political legitimization of their identity's basis and language. Bilingual education in Guatemala plays an important role in shaping the outcome of this process. This may also explain the level of engagement Mayan intellectuals show in their participation in the public life. Thanks to the introduced political changes the question of linguistic diversity and its influence on pan-Mayan and local identity gains in significance in today's Guatemala. Linguistic research, ongoing literacy and raising of the importance of Mayan idioms has led to the emergence of a needed institutional background, which is supposed to strengthen the level of education among Mayas, together with knowledge of a specific language and, in consequence, changes the status of a particular Maya group. To the most effective institutions, who put these tasks as their goals, we may count the Institute of Linguistics, created at the Rafael Landivar University thanks to the actions of Catholic intellectuals gathered around the Instituto Santiago, and the most important of all institutions – Academia de Lenguas Mayas de Guatemala (ALMG). All these institutions employ academic staff well known in world scientific circles and are successful in revitalizing Maya culture. Numerous scientific symposia, linguistic conferences and congresses have mostly also a broader meaning. Thanks to the organization of such events, other Mayan cultural activities are made possible and they contribute to a wider presentation of the current problems of the Maya communities to the ladinos. On the other hand, the Maya themselves do see these linguistic institutions as creating cultural reality and as being defendants of the interests of small indigenous communities on a local and national level. Research interest shown by scholars in these institutions transforms in such cases into political activism, which in consequence leads to the fight for the rights of these communities, especially when linguists see particular Mayan idioms as endangered. For example some of the researchers are focused on presenting the movements acting against the phenomena of native language loss. They postulate a broadening of the context of the linguistic research towards the postcolonial societies in general, as well they include in their research the influence of globalization processes and the incorporation of modern Western patterns into traditional Mayan culture. These phenomena force preventive actions as they tend to become more intense in the future.

Some critics of these initiatives, like the Summer Institute of Linguistics, highlight the leading role of urbanized Mayas in the contemporary activism of this group. The main argument of SIL against them is based on the assumption that a narrow Mayan elite cannot represent the true interests of the rural majority. Furthermore, Mayan activists are being accused of instrumentalizing their cultural traditions to gain casual political support within and outside the country and of reversing old structures and putting, this time, the Mayas on top of an unjust system. This kind of critique is diminished by the Mayan language loyalty movement, as it stresses the rejection of political agenda as its motivation for action. It places also a specific model of multicultural dialogue and co-existence of various ethnic components as the basis for the new Guatemalan democracy. As an example of such a peaceful transition from a militarized regime to democracy, the experience of the Yiddish revitalization movement in Eastern Europe and the Rheato-Romanic language movement in Switzerland are cited. Such a declaration might become more clear when we remember the phenomenon of institutionalized violence in Guatemala, which lasted from the 1950's until 1994. The so called La Violencia is a collective experience of the violent clashes between the leftist guerilla and the government, which took place in the context of the Cold War era and the confrontation between the United States and their allies with the Soviet Union and their satellite states in Eastern Europe, Cuba, and other parts of the world. In most cases the victims of these military actions were the Maya communities, stuck as they were between opposing forces. Memory of the violent past puts therefore a question mark on all the initiatives which deal with the rhetoric of the confrontation. In consequence, the rejection of violence of any kind is a characteristic part of modern Mayan political activism, which tends to stress the need for more cultural, rather than political, solutions of the *status quo*. The revitalization of the Mayan culture is treated as a source of the new national identity, including traditional pre-Colombian customs and the heritage of the Spanish colonizers and their descendants.

The Mayan revitalization movement is being animated nowadays by urban and well educated Mayas. It emphasizes the relation between ethnic identity and language. The modern network of cooperation between various local activists and the leaders of the pan-Mayan movement creates the field for further actions taken on a global scale. It is possible also due to large Mayan diasporas outside Guatemala, for example in the United States. Mayan migrants across the world reveal a common identity, although they still feel attached to their own particular language group in the first place. Their identity structures do not exclude, however, other self-identification levels. On one hand, Mayan migrants show their attachment to other Latin American minorities in countries like United States. Although a large number of them has only little knowledge of Spanish, they often see the link between other Latinos, like the Mexicans or migrants from El Salvador. On the other, as Mayas they express a feeling of belonging to a larger group of all Maya speaking groups, or even of all "indigenous" people. Public expressions of sympathy with Indios from the Amazon, or Mexico are not seldom. Their vision of the world takes into account a specific perspective of a "gaze from below" – a reinterpretation of modern reality from the standpoint of the former inhabitants of the Third World, who now have the opportunity to take part in the public life. The use of the phrase El Mundo Maya ("Mayan World") is taken as an act of proclamation of cultural pride. Modern Mayan identity, no matter if we speak of the Mayas in Guatemala itself or the Mayan diaspora in the US, combines various pieces of cultural references and places in the centre historical roots for contemporary actions. It may be regarded as "living in the past," but these kinds of identity layers are considered by Mayas not as contradictory or artificial. They build a comprehensive structure of their self, constructed from different elements into a hybrid whole.

The significance of language for forming modern Mayan identity may be regarded in several ways. Language functions on a local level as an element contributing to strengthening of the inner ties of the community. It is caused by drawing the shape of the known social order through a common language. For many Mayas, linguistic diversity delivers in this matter useful tools for the process of the self-identification of the group. Local Mayan idioms are perceived as symbolic borderlines of the culturally understandable world, social norms and values, or even the ecological environment. On the other hand, the awareness of the existence of a common Mayan language family and other Maya groups on a non-local level builds the basis for the Mayan revitalization movement in Guatemala. Linguistic identity in this case is equal also to a global identity of indigenous groups living in similar conditions. This discourse on the role of language in creating modern Mayan culture and identity is of course today being put in a specific context of a political and social transition that the country is undergoing at the moment. Nevertheless, it still remains of a cultural character, despite obvious attempts to shift it more towards different groups of interest, political parties and ideologies which have nothing in common with the situation of the Maya.

Chapter 5

Seeing is believing. Anthropological visions of culture

We may agree, with a fair share of certainty, that as long anthropology is lasting, the necessity of "seeing" the cultural *Other* is a constant companion of all ethnographic endeavours. Starting from the beginning of anthropological independence as a discipline, looking upon other people from the ethnographer's stand point has been an important instrument of cognition in its repertoire. Often useful, but sometimes by many also mistrusted, anthropological visions of culture contributed slowly to the building of a much broader world vision; a world beyond the narrow borders of ethnocentric European and Western dogmas. We became aware of the cultural determinations of the world view provided by the eye, or at least of the fact that these limitations exist. It was also constructing the framework of our worldviews through the visualizations of the cultural horizon that we share, as well in attempting to implement it to others. Therefore, the visual aspect of anthropology is the foremost significant factor in understanding how anthropology is contributing to the emergence of a fragile grid of cultural relations which make the foundations of the socio-cultural praxis. The visualization of culture within the anthropological paradigm is also based upon the assumption that culture is characterized by the category of "difference" and that the visual aspect of that inner differentiation is the first to be pointed out in the situation of cultural contact.

The gaze is in this context simultaneously an act of speech. We give names to things and people in the very moment we see them. We give shape to what is culturally indifferent and bring to light what is obscure. By exposing the picture of the *Other* to our eyes, we develop a specific image by using anthropological knowledge as our symbolic camera. However, the anthropological lens uses a harsh light, but a soft focus, to recall the book title by James Peacock.[1] Just like the basic rule of photography, the smaller the aperture, the larger is the depth of field, and anthropology is using its specific optics to gather a vast amount of forms of human cultures in order to get in to focus its object in the broad context upon which it is functioning on an everyday basis. No matter if we speak of exotic customs, rituals, clothes, art, or the way people look or behave, our eyes are the most important tool in the recognition of *otherness* in the first place. As our other senses follow, we slowly build up the picture of the whole – of someone who does not share the same culture as our own. The *Other* is taken into account either through their aesthetical similarity or the lack of it; through implementing our judgement of taste onto structures of values not necessarily covering those shared by ourselves. In this case the category of aesthetic difference is turning into a culturally conditioned axiology. Even more, these aesthetic concepts are sometimes being translated into natural categories, that is, the concepts of the race and racial differentiation of human populations. By combining nature and culture, our visuality is ordering the *Other* into an ontology of the senses. The oppositions emerging from this process have been put forward for a long period of time into terms such as high culture and low culture, civilization and savagery, or simply beauty and ugliness.

If we take classical anthropology and its origins as a product of the transitions in Western thought, we may also trace back the complex process of the visualization of ethnographic knowledge. This process took shape in the midst surrounding the birth of modernity, but it certainly didn't start in the modern age. Cultural curiosity inspiring the collecting of exotic artefacts, or delivering the *Other* to western societies through graphic representations, such as paintings or sketches, was present from the very moment Europeans had acknowledged the fact that their own position is not in the centre of the universe, but that they are just one of many civilizations inhabiting the known world. For the ancient Greeks, just like for example Herodotus, describing the societies of the Middle East and the Mediterranean was just as much important as picturing the Greek military victories over the Persians in the form of *bas-reliefs*. Ancient art wasn't regarded as a dead

[1] See J. L. Peacock, *The Anthropological Lens. Harsh Light, Soft Focus*, Cambridge 2004.

representation of a living reality. Pictures were brought into life through the addition of a specific socio-cultural and political praxis (i.e. rituals) emphasizing the Greek success as a moral and, in consequence, a cultural victory over the barbaric hordes. Thus the visual aspect of culture was in this case dependant on all other spheres of the human cultural agency. It was a part of a vast spectrum of cultural actions, undertaken with the intent to bring it closer to the viewer's experience of it. A pure and sterile image was virtually non-existent without that praxis, that had put it in motion. Ancient art had delivered people a needed relevance to the reality that was surrounding them. In consequence, culture was, back then, visual in the strict sense of the term. It couldn't be deprived of its visual aspect by putting pictures into the framework of art understood as an abstract set of aesthetical ideas and norms. Everything could be seen and looked at by adding our own life experience to the given image and immediately could be grasped by the viewer as reality itself. The distinction between what is real and what is depicted was drawn according not to the ideology behind the image (or the discourse as we would say nowadays), but through the things portrayed. The gods, heroes or other mythical figures represented through ancient art were part of everyday life just as any other personas. Their influence on the way people made their choices, how they acted and what they did was essential in the comprehension of their world view.

Europe in the Middle Ages too, although rejecting most of the ancient aesthetic traditions, did not differ much in this matter. Religion became an instant key to all questions and was regarded as the only source of reality, including visual perception. Even the word of God had to be translated into pictures in order to bring it closer to the masses, when we take into account the low literacy at that time. The religious passion depicted in the church paintings did make the people of that time believe that the final judgement would be brought upon the wicked, sinners, savages, pagans or simply non-Christians. Their only sin was not being one of "us," but the Lord's punishment for being different was certain. There could be only one God, one Church and one valid civilization – a Christian dominion fighting an eternal struggle against infidels. The cultural basis for this assumption was drawn from a single and unquestionable source – the Holy Bible, or to be more specific – the Church's interpretation of it. The historical events that followed (the Protestant revolution for example) showed that even this source could be misleading. On the other hand, the Catholic Church, deprived of its former political power, maintained its cultural influence in the next ages, shaping the anthropological concept of man and culture in strictly religious terms. Of course, the cultural discourse of the Middle Ages and the years after was not anthropological in the contemporary sense of the word. "Anthropos" as a general category was bound by the context surrounding it. This changed with the rise of the Enlightenment and the 19th-century social and philosophical paradigm. The imagery of this time period directed the study of man into the field of universal cultural characteristics shared by all mankind, not just particular cultures. The myth of a "noble savage" did spread across the Western hemisphere and early researchers contributed to its ideological foundations through their basic ethnographic study of the world's cultural diversity by assembling what was regarded as visually interesting. The set of carefully selected cultural items, like material tools or "primitive" art, did quickly fill the shelves in the European museums with various exotic artefacts. Their aesthetic value had been estimated through their similarity to Western counterparts. 19th-century ethnography focused clearly on collecting evidence of the primary role of the white man's culture among existing and past civilizations. The image of the *Other* was pushed into the field of distant historical events that had shaped the contemporary image of humankind, i.e. Western civilization. "Our living ancestors" were pictured as *quasi*-Neolithic communities, in some sort similar to the Europeans, but also full of savagery and violence. The Victorian imaginarium of anthropology was rich in such vague comparisons. Early techniques of capturing the image through daguerreotypes or photography could hardly reflect the cultural reality on the basis of the image alone. Visual anthropology was still in the making at that time. Therefore, the question we have to raise in this context is not just when anthropology became visual, but also who did contribute to this phenomena, how culture had been pictured through the years, and (last but not least) why visualization became a significant issue not just in anthropology itself, but also in other academic domains.

The very moment anthropology opened its eyes as an independent discipline within the humanities was also the moment the Western world had started to look at other cultures from the position of colonial dominance, power and usually also by the application of direct or indirect violence. However, before Victorian anthropology and colonialism had begun to start their own ethnographic enterprises in Africa or India, the study of culture used specific visual methods and data as a tool for a systematic recreation of the existing and past cultural diversity. Of course, the limitations of early 19th-century technology couldn't provide the complete picture of how these objects were used by their owners through photographs, sound recordings or movies, but nevertheless the Museums in London, Paris or Vienna started to be filled with cultural objects from every corner of the world, making it for the viewers much easier to see how the tribes and civilizations outside Europe had changed through the ages until their present form. The *Other* had to be put on display in all its diversity for the bourgeoisie eye to make it more real, possible to grasp, and rationally explained. The historical aspect of the interpretation of these exhibitions is obvious in the light of the ideology of social evolutionism or early positivism. Both approaches were taking the idea that the cultural diversity seen in the museums cabinets has also a natural basis for granted. Again, the aesthetic evaluation of so called primitive art, however also much appealing to the 19th-century artists *milieu*, took over and the rationalization of the category of cultural difference moved onto the field of the natural sciences. The holistic approach of anthropology in its infancy affected the study of culture in terms of race, natural order and development. Western civilization was considered as the most advanced form of the cultural achievement of Man. The picture of the *Other* has gained much in its contrast. Monochrome visions of culture became common and dominant. As George Stocking states, the industrial revolution had put a symbolic mark on what was back then (i.e. traditional societies) and what is now (the Victorian society in Britain for example).[2] Cultural primitivism was exaggerated and over exposed through collections of curiosities – whether the stone tools of Aborigines, Egyptian mummies, or African fetishes. On the other side, cultural development was measured in technology and science; London's Crystal Palace, where these mummies and fetishes were displayed, was a good example of this. It was a clear symbolic self-expression of Western civilizatory and technological domination through architecture and art.

As technological means allowed one to grasp the picture of the anthropological field of research through photography and later also movies, the visual aspect became slowly, but surely, an integral part of the ethnographic description of the cultural universe. The visual paradigm, still bound by the direct experience of an image, was slowly entering the mass production and reproduction pushing it beyond its context of origin. Thus, the image became independent and gained much autonomy. Nevertheless, the best way to look at early 19th-century daguerreotypes was to see them in person.

[2] G. W. Stocking Jr., *Victorian Anthropology*, New York 1987, p. 187.

As this technique is based on putting the image on a silver plate, it may also be taken as a specific Lacanian mirror of the viewer. Civilized Europeans looked at themselves also often through the image of the savage depicted therein. What they did see, was astonishing. A striking resemblance was found in these images, which linked the Europeans with the societies outside Europe through a fragile thread of historical associations. The nature of the main difference between both parties involved was grounded in terms of temporal discrepancy on the level of cultural development and modernization. According to many, the *bon sauvagé* was a direct reflection of an unspecific Neolithic community of the first unnamed Europeans living somewhere in the midst of a distant history. In the eyes of the followers of the Enlightenment philosophy, the "savage within" could be domesticated if only one would reject everything that was irrational, i.e. superstition, magic, religion etc. – that is related to the past. One had to be oriented towards a modernist future, where there was no place left for all of these peculiar artefacts of the primitive past. Science, also social anthropology, was regarded as a tool for this transition, as well its visual aspect was instrumentalized by the ideology of (forced) modernization. Obedience to this positivistic postulate was compulsory and modern visual technology could help to overcome all obstacles. The birth of visual ethnography is closely linked with the emergence of the new media. It is conditioned by the means we are given by the very historical moment we live in. The socio-cultural context of various approaches towards the visual is as much important as the pictures produced by the visual ethnographers themselves. The building of a significant and contextualized relation between the picture and the viewer might be a key factor in reconstructing the critical trajectories of the emergence of visual anthropology and the basic modern visual paradigm in the study of culture.

The photographic journeys of Edward Sheriff Curtis in the American Wild West, by the end of 19th-century deliver a good example how the construction of the image of Native Americans was perceived not just by ethnographers, but also by Curtis's fellow Americans, entering modernity equipped with a set of technological and scientific lenses, which could provide a sharper image and more focused reflection of reality. Curtis's photographs depict American Indians in what was seen as their natural habitat – the great plains of the Mid West, pueblos of the South West or the stony coastal beaches of Alaska with their scattered totem poles. In a kind of mythological narrative Curtis is telling the story of the Sioux or the Navajo in phrases consisting just from images – very much emotional, appealing and truly romantic in their aesthetical and ideological level of interpretation. This does not change the fact that his viewers expected these images to be real. They were made in the heart of the American nation in its making, showing the slowly agonizing native tribes and cultures making room for a new Western civilization. So thought Curtis's clients, like J. P. Morgan, who financed most of his expeditions. Although not a professional anthropologist, the American photographer through his works influenced strongly experts on Native American culture, like his co-worker and friend George Byrd Grinnell. Their fruitful cooperation had made it possible to popularize a specific image (or simply a myth) of the Indians among white Americans. On the other hand, it had also made the foundation for a widespread interest in the indigenous cultures.

Curtis's work published in the years 1907–1930 as the twenty volumes titled "The North American Indian" became without shadow of a doubt an almost instant success. Through placing the images in a carefully described stories telling the lifestyle of the Indians, Curtis managed to fill the image stills with life and to simultaneously gain interest from his readers across the continent, as well from abroad. The image of the *Other*, embraced by many, was slowly settling in the Western world view as a given idea of *Otherness*. The exoticism applied towards this imagery was surely a necessary element for distinguishing between us and them. The picture had won through its contrast. The strongly technological Western world had looked at the *Other* with a feeling of a lost innocence, nobility and pureness that we too had once had. Curtis's photographs had reflected such belonging in a way which is even today regarded as highly aesthetical. His photographs are often found and reproduced nowadays in the form of popular posters, t-shirts or even tattoos. For Curtis himself the American Indian was thus an excellent example of specific processes, which tackled all other indigenous groups and contributed to the vanishing of their culture or sometimes physically the Indian groups themselves due to war, starvation or disease brought by the colonizers. The Indians of the South West became against their will a symbolic recapitulation of the most violent side of 19th-century American history and of the cultural contacts between natives and the whites.

The rising dominance of the occidental view was recaptured by the American photographer by putting the Indians into imaginary frames of traditional culture. For Curtis making pictures was somehow remaking history, or to be more specific – his own view of a very particular past – a past which had moved the indigenous discourse into the area of made up Wild West imagery and not facts. Anthropological picture taking has been quickly distorted into fictional picture making. An interesting aspect of this approach is related to Curtis's own method of work. It is known that every single evidence of modernization of the Indians was removed from the frame, and he was also known for a careful preparation of the photo set and of making all Western artefacts (like clocks, tools or clothing) simply disappear. This kind of falsification of image might be, however, conceptualized in reference to the ideology behind it. His oddly understood perfectionism was at the same time a moral postulate. He and some of his contemporaries were convinced of the importance of rescuing the traditional Indian culture from vanishing. The Sioux or the Navajo were themselves a "vanishing race" and the urgency of capturing precious moments of their genuine indigenous existence was as much important as portraying these people's life in terms that were acceptable and driven away from the early Western anthropological theories of human cultural universalism. As an effect of this, Curtis was reluctant to go into the specific of a particular example, instead making general conclusions on all American Indians and expressing the idea that "all native peoples were a homogenous culture."[3]

In the light of Curtis's work the ethnographic image became at that time an object of a more or less obvious manipulation. Staging scenes by photographers and movie makers for a better look in front of the camera required an intervention in the picture itself. Three of the most known examples of manipulating the cultural reality are related to movies by Louis Buñuel, "Land without bread" and Robert J. Flaherty's "Nanook of the North" and "Man of Aran." These movies are early 20th-century attempts to reflect not quite strict ethnographic data, but to provide a general look at local European cultures and their folklore in an age of a spreading modernity. We may argue, of course, that neither Buñuel nor Flaherty were anthropologists in a strict sense of the word. But Buñuel, a surrealist film maker, and Flaherty a pioneer in film documentary, were using the same ethnographic language for their different causes. Buñuel portrayed a local village on the Spanish-Portuguese border operating with shock, disgust and moral provocation. Flaherty on the other side, imitated anthropological fieldwork. His goal was to present the universal struggle between man and nature. The

[3] M. H. Kennedy, "Introduction," in E. S. Curtis, *The Plains Indian. Photographs of Edward S. Curtis*, Lincoln 2001, p. 4.

Inuit family of Nanook had to fight for its survival in the far north just like the Irish fisher family of the Aran Isles had to undergo their final battle with the sea to maintain their economic existence. Direct interference in the picture is in both cases visible in the falsification of ethnographic data for the sake of an audience-attracting narration.

Changing facts, arranging ceremonies and inserting objects from different cultural contexts became fashionable. It turned into carefully constructed *modus operandi* of visual anthropology at that time. Natural cultural situations and picturing the everyday life of people were transformed to a culturally acceptable aesthetics. Everything had to be just perfect for the Western eye. This affects also the work of Curtis, criticized for obvious image manipulation at both levels in terms of taking the actual picture and post production. Removing modern material artefacts was for Curtis and people of the modern age necessary for recapturing the true nature of the Wild West, where civilization and tradition clashed. American Indians were never wild enough with their horses and plumes, the Pygmies of Congo never archaic enough with their bows and stone axes, and the Trobriand Islanders never exotic enough with their ceremonial masks and pearl necklaces. This iconography of *otherness* was interpreted as a symbolic triumph of civilization over savagery; a visual domination taking place along with the military, political and economic conquest of non-Westerners. Colonialism was extended in this manner into the visual sphere.

This problem, tackled by Edward Said in his book "Orientalism," is even more emphasized in the analysis by James Clifford of Marcel Griaule's ethnographic praxis in Africa in the 1930's.[4] What is significant here is that Griaule, a leading figure in French ethnology beside Michel Leiris, had developed a specific concept of fieldwork – "a documentary system [governed by images of collection, observation, and interrogation] and a initiatory complex [where dialogical processes of education and exegesis come to the fore]." These two approaches were perceived by Griaule as complementary. The shift from collecting the images to understanding the meaning of them was a smooth transgression from the imperial gaze to intercultural dialogue. During his Dakar-Djibouti and Mali missions, Griaule collected a large number of photographs, which are now gathered in the *Musee de L'Homme* in Paris. These images were for him not just dead objects; a final product of the

4 See J. Clifford, "Power and Dialogue in Ethnography. Marcel Griaule's Initiation," in G. W. Stocking Jr. (ed.), *Observers Observed. Essays on Ethnographic Fieldwork*, Madison & London 1983.

anthropological fieldwork put in a static exposition. They might be brought to life again by the reconstruction of a cultural map of the human terrain. The cartographic metaphor is here accurate in the sense of Griaule's work as an aerial spotter before his ethnological career. In his case the colonial eye isn't that harsh as Said would like to see. It is the absolute gaze from above. The visual data and observation has in the French scholar's view much more potential to deliver an adequate amount of information on African cultures as interviews done in the field, according to him an uncertain form of oral collaboration. Griaule points out the assumption that the image brings the "edge needed to provoke, control, and verify confessional discourses." It delivers the clarity of cultural relations, and in the context of the colonial French rule over a large part of Africa this works both ways. Griaule observes and photographs the Dogon, and, as he witnessed, the natives are following his every step with their eyes. Nevertheless, this mutual observation was far from equality. It was a drama of an application of colonial power and forcing obedience, more a situation of George Orwell's experience as a colonial police officer killing the infamous elephant than Clifford Geertz's participation in a Balinese cock fight. Compulsive capturing of the images was for Griaule the first step in a controlled process of revealing culture's hidden secrets.

With the decline of the colonial system, the vanishing of its traditional object of interest (traditional societies), and the processes of globalization, anthropology shifted from the study of particular cultures in their local environments to questions on culture of a more philosophical nature. So too did its visual sub-discipline. Thus, culture became an issue understood in terms of the subjective experience of the people captured in the photographs and film. The experiment undertaken by Sol Worth and John Adair in 1966 by handing out 16mm cameras to the Navajo Indians, previously teaching them to use this equipment, has shown an existing gap in what anthropologists see and what is perceived by their native interlocutors. The same issue is raised in the ethnographic cinema of Jean Rouch or Tim Asch. However, the image of the *Other* today has become blurred and dynamic. The more we want it to stay still in the frame, the more it is unreachable. The desire to get it in order, to structure the existing cultural phenomena by freezing the moment on tape, and to digitalize the visual data, isn't over yet. As we come to the question why anthropology is still attached to this wishful way of thinking, we may ask ourselves if anthropology can be ever deprived of its eyes at all. Seeing is believing, as visual recapturing of foreign rituals and customs brings them closer into our own cultural home; it makes the *Other* if not our close neighbour and friend, then at least someone who's way of living we acknowledge. The important difference between today and the early visualizations of cultures by Edward Curtis, Bronisław Malinowski and later by Gregory Bateson and John Collier, lies upon the ideology behind ethnographic images. As Jean Rouch mentions in one of his interviews visual anthropology shares an uncertain future, but it will survive as long as the production of ethnographic imagery does not become purely technical and will maintain its link to reality. Symbols are meaningless without the practice which puts them in to motion. The practice of anthropology is what anthropologists do, as James Peacock says. The practice of the image is to be seen and the visions of culture delivered by anthropology perform still quite well despite their more or less obvious limitations.

Today, visual anthropology (ethnography) is a well established sub-discipline with a wide range of interest areas and a rich cognitive toolbox. Visualizing ethnographic knowledge is regarded even today as an important and often necessary part of the enterprise by a large group of fieldworkers. This omni-presence of the "visual" in anthropology is certainly an effect of the past debates and polemics on the nature of the anthropological work and its object of study, but it is also the consequence of the anthropological practice itself. The act of cognition is always linked with the senses. Understanding how the cultural *Other* thinks, acts and feels involves the sensory machinery we all posses and allows it to establish a close relation to what is out there by seeing, smelling, touching and hearing. Of course, these senses may function both ways; they shape our image of reality through delivering empirical data our minds are able to process, but on the other hand due to their imperfection they are a boundary we will probably never fully cross. Human beings are sentenced therefore to life in the sensory "Panopticon" of seeing others and ourselves through the bars of social roles, cultural values and institutions. In this context the visual aspect of "doing" anthropology in the field is related to the somehow aesthetic evaluation of these fields of our existence and a visual translation into our own terms, symbols and metaphors. We simply cannot leave behind what is culturally determined. Our cultural glasses are accompanying us through all stages of life and in all of our actions, shaping them through our motivating agency on the basis of particular cultural ideologies.

Being aware of our ethnocentric evaluation and culturally limited worldview is certainly new to some research/researchers, and surely not widely accepted in the public sphere in countries with an homogenous cultural structure (or rather a popular view of a national monolithic community), which is very much the case of Poland for example. The aim of anthropological research in this case is often to highlight the real cultural diversity of these societies, carefully hidden by recent history (in Eastern Europe the time of the communist regimes), as well contemporary or future processes which will involve these societies in confronting and acknowledging the presence of the *Other*. Visualizing cultural diversity makes probably the attempts to apply anthropological knowledge a much easier task, or at least it allows to make the first move in the right direction.

Bringing together again anthropology and its related fields through the visual component has to include a vast discourse, which is being associated with this issue. As the methodology of visual anthropology has gained much attention through the works of such authors as Sarah Pink, Jay Ruby, Marcus Banks, or John Collier, its theoretical foundations are still at stake. The light of the visual discourse is in this scientific domain scattered with polemical debates on what anthropology is allowed to do, and what should be left as it is. It's a key issue in today's anthropology, and not just in relation to its visual sphere. Subjective engagement of the researcher when conducting fieldwork is regarded by some as an unnecessary and dangerous, and thus leading to the falsification of ethnographic data. Our own eyes cannot be trusted anymore. A radical disconnection is needed, a groundbreaking de-visualization of anthropology, which could save the day (scientific objectivism) – as some of the critics say. This kind of critique, however, does not see the close link of contemporary cultural processes with the visual basis. The presence of new media and visual technologies seem to expand the range of references of human agency in contemporary culture, especially when we speak of its global character. If the postulated de-visualization would be considered as a part of modern anthropology, it might find some attention among those scholars who are fundamentally grounded in the critical issues mentioned above. If seeing the *Other* equals believing in our anthropological knowledge, it also means that the awareness of the limitations to our scientific eyes is as much important as the effort to produce a paradigm, one that does not impose any power onto the people's lives in terms of repression and dominance as it has in the past.

Part II

Culture and religion in the age of global change

Chapter 6

Domestication of the Orient. Dimensions of the cultural perception of religious otherness in contemporary Europe

Today, the collective representations of the Orient, including all issues related to one of the largest Eastern religions of the world, i.e. Islam, are burdened with a quite unequivocal geopolitical context. Nowadays, the global dimension and range of both the political and military aftermath of actions resulting from the events of September 11, 2001, are one of the most common points of reference in the case of the problem of the Orient, or, to put this in a broader perspective, of cultural and religious otherness in general. Popular associations related to all areas located to the east of the border of the so-called Western World are now being defined by the matter of Muslim fundamentalism and extremist movements of eastern provenance. Today, this kind of cultural categorisation of the world constitutes one of the ruling models of the typical thinking of a Westerner, or at least of those parts of Western societies that identify with the Euro-Atlantic Judeo-Christian tradition. Thus, in a world built in this way, there is not much space for cultural otherness that goes far beyond the European representations of the religious drive, and a considerable part of the forms of Islam can be counted among them.

What underlies this phenomenon is certainly not only a lack of openness to a foreign culture, but also, to a larger extent, a result of some deeply rooted cultural stereotypes. It is these stereotypes on which the various images of reality, which are not entirely true, are most frequently created and reinforced. They are also often transferred into the sphere of religiousness, at times becoming a seedbed for cultural misunderstanding and outright conflicts. For many years, European Christianity and the Orient, strongly dominated by the Muslim element, have remained in ambivalent relations towards each other and the differences in their perception of the world in terms of religion has impelled representatives of both cultures to mutual suspiciousness. The complex network of relations that link both civilisations in the sphere of religious disputes between Christian theology and Islamic religious reflection remains, of course, in close relation to other levels of the situation of contact (economy, politics, etc.). However, this contact is to a large extent marked by the clashes between both religious systems and it is the issue of difference in expressing one's own religiousness that seems to emanate onto the remaining aspects of this problem.

The problem of the schematic image of the Orient and the ways of structuring such images has been present in scientific discourse for at least several decades. The beginnings of the reflection on this topic date back directly to the middle of the 20th-century and are unequivocally related to the cultural and political context of that time. A problem is posed by the process of the erosion of the European colonial system. This process, initiated first by India and Pakistan, and then also the vast majority of African countries gaining independence, forms the basic point of reference in the debate on the presence of the so-called East in contemporary Western collective representations. In the 1960s in Europe, the social perception of the decolonisation process was received in terms of ethnic and cultural emancipation. Of course, the slogans of the emancipation of social, cultural and ethnic groups used to be received as part of a broader phenomenon of social change and the counterculture actions of the young generation in those years. Notwithstanding this, the fact of the old colonies gaining even some nominal independence entailed a series of other social phenomena, such as the considerable inflow of immigrants from outside Europe. Thus, the inhabitants of the Old Continent had to face a totally new situation. Using the categories known to them, Europeans strove to put the new *status quo* in order, attempting to create a system of values that would be understandable to them. The thing is, however, that the new system of values included only the Western cognitive categories and, what is most important, moral categories as well. The behaviour of newcomers from Pakistan or from Arab countries seemed to be something totally incomprehensible tofor the average inhabitant of Britain or the Netherlands. They aroused surprise and, in extreme cases, even outright hostility. European nationalist movements established after World War II only fuelled the xenophobic attitudes by proclaiming anti-immigrant slogans veiled into the fight for the protection of the national identity of Western societies.

However, in order to understand the growth of a mass dislike for newcomers from the countries of the Orient, it is required to examine in the first place the process of changing social attitudes in European countries with regard to cultural and religious otherness. Insofar as there was a far-reaching opening to foreign culture (at least at a declarative level) in the 1960s, today we can observe a clear negation of that model. In this regard, the events of September 11 do not constitute any particular turning point in time. Notwithstanding this, they are a significant expression of transformations against both Islam and the East in general. The cases of attacks on mosques and Muslim institutions, as well as the Muslims themselves, have become a more frequently observed phenomenon than they used to be only a few years ago. These cases aroused a strong commotion among the followers of the multicultural model and the very policy of multiculturalism. The shock that fell to the lot of these groups consisted mainly in realising the need for articulating the fact of a crisis of the policy to date. As a result, Western societies on both sides of the Atlantic had to face the problem of redefining their own attitudes towards the world of Islam, as well as towards the broadly defined representatives of the broadly defined Orient.

The category of the Orient, including its perception in religious terms, has been present in Western culture for many centuries. However, it was not before the 20th-century that it gained new importance. In this respect, the fundamental point of reference is the work of the Palestinian political scientist, literary critic and political activist, Edward W. Said, entitled *Orientalism* (1978). This book is undoubtedly a fundamental work within the scope of cultural studies and for some people it constitutes one of the most important scientific books published in the second half of the 20th-century. In the book, Said conducts a detailed reconstruction of the process of the symbolic structuring of the Orient as a peculiar, as well as an essentially false ontological category of the Western world. His starting point is the conviction that the symbolic domination of the West over the East is continual. The Palestinian intellectual persists in a thesis which claims that the relations between the Western cultural area and the Orient are marked by an insistent desire of Westerners to subjugate and dominate all what is associated with the East. This relation of the imperialist appropriation of the Orient was supposed to have originated at the turn of the 18th and 19th-century and its consequences can still be felt in the relations between Europe and the countries, for instance, of the Middle East. Such a deep dependence of relations between both civilisation circles finds its ground in the sense of bringing the Enlightenment thought and, what follows, also the European moral, aesthetic and religious values, as well as manners, to many other corners of the globe – it is a sense that has been growing in European societies since the end of the 18th-century. For a Westerner, the Orient becomes a representation. In other words, instead of the Orient itself, it is a Western representation of the Orient structured on the basis of Western categories. In Said's opinion, the majority of cases of attempts to imply Christian ethics to the communities inhabiting Oriental countries, or countries regarded as such by Westerners, led to the situation of conflict, simultaneously constituting somewhat of a justification for the imperial policy.

Said extends these theses not only to the area of the Middle East, which is close to him, but also to all areas of the world that have been affected by the process of colonisation. This measure becomes more comprehensible if we consider the fact that today Said is believed to be the leading representative of the so-called post-colonial theory. However, both Said's work and his views constitute an extraordinarily original project within the scope of cultural criticism and social analysis. What makes his theses enjoy such popularity among many researchers of social phenomena is the fact of their going beyond the cultural and political discourse and transferring the problem of colonial dependence and its manifestations onto the field of systemic theory.

As Said claims in the opening lines of his theoretical considerations on Orientalism: "[...] my study hitherto has tried to describe *the economy* that makes Orientalism a coherent subject matter."[1] This statement makes the concept of Orientalism promoted by the author bear the marks of a peculiar social and cultural phenomenon in the sense of Durkheim's social fact. Thus, it is a notion that allows itself to be conceptually caught in the limits of social and cultural metaphors and references, which are transformed into social facts at their next stage. It is an element of the structure including historical, cultural and political relations between the Orient and the Occident. There-

[1] E. Said, *Orientalism. Western Conceptions of the Orient*, London 1995, p. 202.

fore, the historical outline of the relations between these areas of culture is so important for Said. It is precisely because of the reproduction of the cultural representation of the Orient by Westerners in the course of history that its essentially false image has been so strongly rooted in the Western thought. The European art of the 19th-century developed even a specialised trend in painting, called Orientalism, which has largely contributed to creating a certain set of associations with the East. These associations were of an aesthetic nature in the first place and they found their justification in the artistic and literary traditions of the Occident. In this regard, Oriental paintings most often referred to feminine motifs, sublime eroticism and superficial references to Islam. In Said's opinion, the image of the Orient shaped in such a manner functions until the present day in the collective consciousness of many Western societies. Based on the imperial doctrine, the political actions towards Oriental societies seem only to confirm the thesis Said keeps repeating, namely, that Europe, together with the United States, have still not freed themselves from their schematic thinking of this type. Therefore, "[...] Orientalism can thus be regarded as a manner of regularized (or Orientalized) writing, vision and study, dominated by imperatives, perspectives, and ideological biases ostensibly suited to the Orient."[2]

Post-colonial studies and Said's concept of Orientalism have set a direction in the research of cultural transformations that has gained a number of followers, as well as they became subject to criticism. As far as the latter criticism is concerned, it is required to mention Robert Irwin's work entitled "Dangerous Knowledge," where the author reproaches Said for his using far-fetched simplifications and his schematism of thinking. Notwithstanding this, the analysis of social phenomena in the global dimension from the point of view of post-colonial studies incorporates an interesting, albeit probably not too innovative, assumption. It indicates the existence of certain mechanisms of cultural identification in the relations between disparate circles of civilisation, mainly in the context of the process of structuring collective identities.

As a certain counterpoint to Said's concept of Orientalism, it is possible to adduce here the theses of Samuel Huntington, published in his famous work entitled "The Clash of Civilizations and the Remaking of World Order" (1996). Simplifying the issues to a large extent, one could say that the Huntingtonian model of the geopolitical structure of the world assumes the existence of certain supranational areas of civilisation, where cultural values

---

[2] Ibidem, p. 202.

(including religion), political interests and development models are extremely out of tune. In time, this model makes the societies belonging to them pursue their own goals, i.e. a situation of conflict and confrontation. Thus, this view constitutes somewhat of a confirmation of Said's theses. They have also become the target of the criticism of followers of post-colonial studies, with Said on top, accusing the American political scientists of using Western stereotypes of thinking about the cultural order of the world. These charges, preferred in the context of conflict in the Middle East, emphasised the fact that the Huntingtonian model was out of tune with many situations, where the relations between the Western and the Eastern circles of civilisation were taking place, first and foremost, on a completely different level and, secondly, they had the character of a complementary supplementation to both cultures at the systemic level.

One of the cases of such a complex cultural entanglement might be the unique cultural character of the Mediterranean Sea basin, particularly in the south of Spain, where the presence of the Arab culture is still visible today as well. The existence of the Granada caliphate in the region of Andalucía ended together with the Christian Reconquista of the 15th-century. However, its presence has been inscribed for good in the so-called cultural landscape of the region. It is perhaps because of its historical proximity to the civilisation of the Orient and the influence of the culture of Islam that this part of Europe demonstrates a much higher level of openness to religious otherness. Thus, the Muslim community inhabiting the south of Spain and France forms there an integral part of the social system instead of a foreign element, in relation to which the rest of the society in these countries is positioned. Of course, the case of Andalucía is only a tiny segment of the whole problem of the presence of the Orient in the social awareness in the West. Nevertheless, it makes the mechanism of the social categorisation of the East as a place that constitutes a counterbalance for the Christian Europe become less "rigid" in its ontological aspirations to explain the world. Historical relations are also not the main determinant of the form of the symbolic representation of the East, in spite of their significant importance for the awareness of the people living in these regions. On the other hand, the discourse of everyday life seems to be a factor of this type.

The process of bestowing certain traits and attributes upon the Orient is a process which is constituted in contemporary Europe by actions in the field of public discourse. The image of the East created in the media, popular literature and everyday relations is most often described with the radicalisation of the Westerners' social views and attitudes towards a real or imaginary Islamic fundamentalism.

At present, direct associations with Islam and the cultures of the Orient set the path for the social representations of Westerners, most often towards such notions as religious fundamentalism, women's rights, economic and civilisation backwardness, etc. In the media coverage, what we most often see is women in burkas, strolling between stalls in Afghan cities, demonstrations of Hezbollah followers, or the streets of Baghdad in ruin. The associations of a recipient of these images are headed in one direction and essentially what is perhaps originally intended to deliver knowledge of the world becomes a mechanical reproduction of certain patterns of thinking about the East. Thus, the Orient, regardless of whether it is associated with the Middle East or the area of eastern Asia, is received in a context accurately set by pop culture and the extra-scientific discourse. Hearing the slogan "fundamentalism," we automatically direct our thoughts towards the extreme splinter groups of Islam in their most radical form, i.e. wahabitism. This type of Western thinking also finds its reflection in language and the semiotic categories that constitute the basis for the Orientalism described by Said. Publicly expressed anxiety against cultural foreignness, fuelled by disturbing news from the East, is present in the language used both in the media and in the works of authors who call themselves intellectuals, or who are commonly deemed so.

In this regard, it is required to recall, for instance, the recently deceased Italian journalist Oriana Fallaci, whose texts and newspaper reports enjoyed high popularity at some time in the past, not only in Italy, but also among European intellectuals (what is interesting, they were mainly associated with the liberal and democratic option). It was all the more surprising to see the publication of the text entitled "The Rage and The Pride," dedicated to her personal judgements towards the growing wave of newcomers, mainly from Arab countries, whom she perceived as making a real invasion of the Old Continent. In this text, Fallaci reveals, to the surprise of her fans to date, her deep dislike for people who, in her opinion, destroy Florence, the symbol of European high culture. At this point, Fallaci expresses all the possible stereotypes concerning the Orient, which are so fiercely denounced by representatives of the so-called post-colonial theory. Arab immigrants are people of incomprehensible customs, lack of manners and respect for the significance of the place they are in and, first and foremost, they are not willing to express their gratitude in a servile manner towards a society that had welcomed them with open arms. In the opinion of some people, the Italian journalist merely expressed a view shared by the majority of Europeans, especially those who live in societies that pursue the policy of cultural pluralism and the significant part of whom is a minority of Oriental origin. The dislike for Islam, or the European representation of Islam, forms an important part of this reasoning. The view shared by Fallaci that Europe is at the crossroads at the moment, and that it has to define its Christian identity unequivocally, results from the conviction that European culture is monolithic in character and its relational dimension is persistently negated. The criticism that came down on Fallaci from liberal intellectuals, human rights protection movements and Islamic organisations indicated, first of all, the language of outright conflict which has been present in the last texts written by the Italian writer. Agitating for war with what Fallaci deems a manifestation of Islamic fundamentalism translates in itself into an expression of fundamentalist views. Admittedly, she is far from the contemporary Christian fundamentalism observed in America, or the movement of the so-called "born-again Christians" (which the former President of the USA, George W. Bush identifies with, for instance). Notwithstanding this, the voice of this author is close to the rules which fundamentalist religious thinking is based on.

However, in order to understand the scale of such a radical reception of the fact of the intensified wave of immigrants from the area of the Orient, it would be appropriate to answer the question of whether the attitude presented by Fallaci is merely an expression of a marginal political and social view, or maybe it is an indication of a broader phenomenon. Some help in this regard might be provided by the text by the Syrian researcher of religious phenomena who creates his works in Germany – Bassam Tibi. The following sentence, contained in his book entitled "Der Religiöse Fundamentalismus im Übergang zum 21. Jahrhundert," shows us how deeply fundamentalism is associated with Islam in the Western reasoning and, what follows, why it is perceived as a threat to the Western democracies. As Tibi states, "[...] both civilizations are being characterized by a universalistic understanding of the world, along which are related separate ideas of world order, and these tend clearly to clash" and further on he also states that: "[...] Islam and the West are filling these ideas with contradictory content. If we make them political and articulate them in a fundamentalist language, they will gain a neoabsolutist character, and what follows, building bridges between civilizations will become impossible."[3] As we can see, the

[3] Polish translation: B. Tibi, *Fundamentalizm religijny*, Warsaw 1997, p. 71.

above is tantamount to a view that if we speak of the clash between the culture of Islam and the culture of the West, which can be observed today, it is a clash of two fundamentalisms understood as opposing ideological systems. At this point, the ideology of Islamic religious fundamentalism is contrasted with even not so much of a Christian fundamentalism, but rather with the absolutist inclinations of the Western rationalism that stems from the Enlightenment thought. As Horkheimer and Adorno preferred to see it, for instance, Tibi is another author to point out the fact that it is the Enlightenment heritage of absolute reason that gave birth to the attitudes described here, and it is also an indirect cause of the lack of understanding between both civilisations. The combination of the fundamentalist scheme of connecting religious categories and politics proper is to be common to an equal extent to both the so-called hard-liners of European politics and the members of the terrorist organisations from the Middle East. However, it is not merely a clash between two extremities, or a merely oppositional presentation of political extremisms that polarise the contemporary world. At this point, Tibi indicates the connection between religious fundamentalism and Islamic terrorism, which is important for the shape of the present relations between the worlds of the Christian and Islamic traditions. The Europeans often identify the neo-traditionalist ideologies present in Islamic fundamentalism with the culture of Islam as such. As a result, it makes Islam appear as a combative religion based on the idea of Jihad (Holy War), understood literally.

Of course, the problem of the schematisation of the relations presented above is far more complex than the fields of scientific and extra-scientific discourse, outlined here in their general forms. The fact still remains, however, that the Western and Eastern ways of perceiving religious differences result to a large extent from strictly defined and culturally sanctioned stereotypes. The schematic model of religious thinking is peculiar not only to the fundamentalist movements described by Tibi, but also to Western societies in general, as well as to the inhabitants of the so-called Orient. A certain solution to this problem seems to be assuming an attitude that combines a skilful and "understanding" arousal of interest in other religious systems, while simultaneously and unequivocally defining our own religious identity.

Chapter 7

Between Kwanzaa and Jediism. Contemporary constructions of religious identity and imagined communities

By looking at the forms which modern religious identity is taking today, it is not easy to point out its simple shape. In many cases both religious systems and identity locate their doctrinal basis within the pop-cultural sphere, or cultural areas which are far removed from the patterns associated usually with religiosity. More and more often sources of religiosity are being perceived by people as the basis of their own (individual and group) identity in relation to phenomena, being a product of the melting of various religious contents together and used for constructing the category of religiosity around socio-cultural phenomena previously not associated with religion. I would like to dedicate this article to this very issue, which seems today to gain very much attention. Doctrinal constructivism, as it may otherwise be termed, is visible in many new religious phenomena, especially those which win supporters in the western world. New religious movements are being built often within particular discourses and cultural contexts which are a consequence of globalization processes, but which also function as an ideological platform for political postulates (like emancipation rights for various minority groups for example). On the other hand, new religious movements create a specific superstructure for the pop-cultural and media phenomena, like film narratives. Both dimensions of this new religiosity are, however, grounded in a specific system of values, in which the community aspects are being presented as the major issue. Despite the fact that aiming for a life in a group joined by the same religious identity isn't anything new, the constitutive feature of the new types of religiosity in this dimension is their relating to the community aspect in a reflexive manner and openly using socio-cultural symbolism to highlight the selected aspects of identity itself.

This phenomenon might be regarded as a specific consequence of modernism. By recalling a well known work of Anthony Giddens[1] it is worth contemplating if modernity, understood as a kind of worldview system, is not implemented in contemporary religious narratives. The British sociologist claims that the clash with tradition is inscribed within the concept of modernity. Questioning the existing thought systems, including religions, does affect the search for alternative forms of self-realization. Rejecting stiff ideologies is therefore not just a form of contestation, but also an attempt to highlight our position in a constantly changing world. The dynamics of the processes of change do force us to adapt to existing conditions, but also stimulates our change in views and approaches. Modern religious worldviews are in this light a reflection of valid trends and the direction of contemporary culture. Contrary to a popular belief saying that globalization is changing modern societies into homogenous wholes oriented only towards the hedonistic consumption of goods and meanings, the cultural pattern dominating today is a heterogeneous construction as to the content it is based on. An evidence of this tendency might be the more and more popular idea of glocalization, which accepts the inevitable global character of social, cultural and economic ties in the modern world, and at the same time points out that the category of the local and the belonging to local communities is still very much alive and kicking. The eclectics of this form is being expressed also in the way people search today for new spirituality. The diverse array of churches and denominations might seem astonishing when we look closer at the doctrinal inspirations behind those movements. Starting from the widely understood New Age movement, through various groups gathering together UFO believers and ending with the movement of the fictional and cinematic religion of the Jedi Order – they all seem to share a common idea behind those exotic beliefs, i.e. striving for an expressing of a religious identity with the inclusion of the individual character of the religious experience.

A question therefore must be raised – if modern religious movements are oriented at the individual and private aspect of religiosity, why do people still create successful functioning religious institutions and churches? The answer might be related to the issue pointed out by many researchers as a specific

[1] A. Giddens, *The Consequences of Modernity*, Cambridge 1990.

understanding of the category of community, its being one of the ideological premises of the doctrinal systems of those movements. The community of believers is being understood often not just as a group of people, but also as an ideological community. It builds at the same time a community of thoughts and worldviews, which are shared but also cannot be expressed *explicite* by individual who are in fact outside the official churches. It is especially related to people who share a common type of ethics. The mechanism of inclusion is in this case a phenomenon hidden below the apparent surface of the exclusivism of belonging to such groups. Perceiving others as potential members of these communities does, however, require certain fundaments, which are frequently found in the doctrinal principles of those religious movements: an intensive proselytism, actions popularizing those movements in the media and the politics of "public relations" often accompany the existing denominations and those recently emerging. What is interesting such actions usually are not a generally formulated directive existing in the sphere of the worldview, but carefully thought out marketing strategies, just like in the case of other modern organizations focused on attracting more supporters.

Reflexivity of actions has been replaced with a cool costs and risk calculation The rationalization of the code of conduct of the movement's management and its regular members seems to be a constant tendency of many new religious formations. This results from the condition of the contemporary world, in which rationalization and the mechanical aspect of agency is an inalienable part of the human experience. According to Daniel Bell, it is to the same extent the effect of a change in the awareness of the Western societies as valid cosmologies.[2] The postindustrial world order demands to work out such strategies which assure individuals and institutions not just endurance, but also profit and the possibility of its consumption. Excellent examples in this case might be the Church of Scientology or the Amway organization. Special interest, however, might be deserved by those movements which propose to their followers much more than purely material wealth in the earthly life or its more spiritual equivalent in life after death. I mean here religious organizations relating to a specific cultural identity, which apparently has nothing in common with religiosity.

The construction of religious identity is in this case a product of a multidimensional process of self-identification within bigger socio-cultural entities. Members of these movements do identify with a certain position in their

[2] D. Bell, *The Cultural Contradictions of Capitalism*, New York 2008, p. 184.

structure. It is significant that every time we recall such an entity it is being undermined as an expression of a specific order that is only an ideological myth, absolutely non-valid for the contemporary globalized reality. Using such terms as nation or nation state is considered as false from the methodological standpoint, because of the fact that the concept of nation is long passé. Furthermore, binding together the category of national community and religiosity demonstrates, according to such authors like Ernest Gellner, a disturbing close relation to religious fundamentalism.

Gellner's views in the question of the transitions of modern forms of religiosity have to be taken in the context of his standpoint on the changes in modern reality. Gellner, widely known as one of the most sworn critics of treating the idea of postmodernism as a given objectivity, comprehends the direction of changes in modern religiosity in relation to transformations in Western rationality. In his opinion, the process of shaping fundamentalist approaches in many societies is a consequence of translating economic rationality into the language of religion. Radical religious attitudes do go hand in hand with political extremism, which in the Western world frequently uses a language similar to that used in religious discourses. However, in the view of the British scholar, fundamentalism does not reveal itself only in those spheres of our lives which are subjected to the influence of religion. Gellner introduces the term "rational fundamentalism" to describe ideological attitudes (and also research attitudes), which he himself isn't a stranger to.[3] He admits that "the relation between ideology and political order did undergo many historical phases. First in the pre-axis era religion through dance reflected social order: it was a choreography of social relations, it underlined and sanctioned it."[4] This interdependence of both levels ended, however, with the beginning of modernity, but the scope of reason and economic rationality did not push this significant relation out of the human area of agency. What did change, was the emergence of new Enlightenment frames of worldviews. The overlap of these two orders of thinking contributed to a cognitive dissonance. Today, religious fundamentalism occurs everywhere where people cannot define themselves when facing the changing reality. By grasping the vanishing axioms, they radicalize their views and actions, hoping that at least their position in the world of social unrest will remain intact.

In a similar manner this problem is being tackled by another researcher of the phenomenon of religious fundamentalism, Bassam Tibi. This German

[3] E. Gellner, *Postmodernism, Reason and Religion*, New York 1992, p. 105.

[4] Ibidem, p. 116.

scholar, just like Gellner, has the point of view that today's fundamentalisms are closely related to the world of politics and the economy. Despite the apparent distance of the fundamentalist language from the purely material issues, both worlds are similar, because "fundamenalists do not praise the love of God, but strive to take power."[5] It is characteristic that the popularity of various fundamentalisms grows along with the fragmentarization and stratification of everyday life. This specific world "disorder" causes conflicts, driven among others by fundamentalisms. The confrontation does occur frequently in the most extreme points, and therefore the polarization of views matches Huntington's model of the "clash of civilizations." The idea of a community is one of many which could serve as a point of reference for the feeling of ontological security. The contemporary use of the term is, however, carrying the burden of radicalism. So, if we speak of fundemantalism on the religious level, so in the case of community we may speak of nationalism.

We know that these ideologies do not have to exclude each other, and even may construct together a coherent worldview system. As an example here may serve the phenomenon of the frankly said marginal, but without any shadow of a doubt the most colorful, variants of nazi ideology known as nazi esotericism, or nazi occultism. The advocates of these occult options constructed their worldview on the basis of a mythologized history of the German nation, simultaneously creating a system of a *quasi*-religious affirmation of German history. There was a concept of a community present – even more, it was put in the first place. However, it is not this from today's perspective peculiar marriage that seems to be important, but the mechanism of its construction. German nationalism, both in its classical form, as well as the form visible in the nazi ideology, reflected a vision of community which has its roots in the German romantic philosophy of the end of the 18th and beginning of the 19th-century. Along with its rising popularity we could observe the beginning of the consolidation of the German state. Both processes: the birth of national consciousness and the formulation of the thesis that a unified German spirituality exists, tackled identity issues. The view shared by many Germans at the beginning of the 19th-century that the national community has its roots beyond the empirically graspable reality was at the same time an expression of faith in the notion that it is being bound by deeper relations than simple belonging. National identity became at that time a religious and magic identity expressed best in the theses of ariosophy or nazi occultism.

[5] B. Tibi, *Fundamentalizm religijny*, Warsaw 1997, p. 146.

The translation of the supernatural order into the language of politics is happening at an ideological level. That's why we may say that the type of community we speak about is rather an "imagined community" than based on solid premises. We owe the notion of such an imagined community, gaining much popularity these days, to Benedict Anderson. His own concept of imagined community, which one may find in his book from 1983, is related fore mostly to the rule of social constructivism, clearly seen in many national discourses. As an imagined community Anderson describes the product of certain ideological processes, which takes shape as a specific group consciousness. It is based on the conviction that the community created by the group may have not clearly drawn borders (though it may be open to potential new members), but very clear drawn criteria of belonging. This model is related to those types of national consciousness which are specific for groups emerging from other national or ethnic entities, striving to stress their sovereignty, giving the mark of authenticity to their political postulates and strengthening the framework of a group identity. To the set of factors shaping an imagined community we may count in: shared cultural roots, political goals, time perception and religion. The last factor is one of two, beside the dynastic monarchy, cultural systems shaping the foundations of these imagined communities.

The religious fundaments of imagined communities may be determined on the basis of their linguistic manifestations. This also counts in the process of a specific sacralization of language. Despite the fact that the traditional model of community also did use a sacred language, in this case we see a clear difference. As Anderson states: "this kind of classic communities bound together by scared languages did differ from imagined communities, i.e. modern nations. One of significant differences was the conviction of these old communities that the only sacred language is their own, that is also their concepts of belonging to a community."[6] Anderson adds, however, that such a narrative featuring of the concept of a community has certain limitations. Language is dependent on the change of the character of the sign itself which becomes the object of ideological agency. For an imagined community to exist through submerging it in cultural symbols, it is necessary to give the signs a non arbitrary character. This thought is supposed to be unfamiliar to the nature of Western culture, where the flexibility of symbol

[6] B. Anderson, *Imagined Communities. Reflections on the Origin and Spread of Nationalism*, New York – London 2006, p. 27.

use and its semantic connotations is relatively big. Such problems the communities outside the Western world do not have, for they treat language (for example Chinese ideograms) as a reflection of reality and not its freely fabricated representation. This causes that in the linguistic sphere imagined communities strive to give the signs of authenticity to phenomena from a symbolic space.

Anderson's concept finds application in those religious movements which function within the frames of particular discourses of modernity. If we assume after David Howarth that a discourse is being made by a set of objects and actions having an attached meaning and being a product of historically conditioned systems of rules, then the cultural narratives created by those movements operate with signs related to certain steady points in the framed reality (or just try to make such an impression). This might be made by such spheres as sexual identity, race or the media. In the case of the media sphere, the basis for constructing identity is taking for example cinematographic fiction as reality. The common denominator of the organizations mentioned here is, however, the striving to "close ranks" through the stressing of their community character. The often expressed aversion towards treating them as formal religious institutions or churches goes hand in hand with the publicly stressed defining of them as "social movements" or "subcultures." Both terms may be treated as two poles of the same idea of community, and the mechanism of self-identification of their members as two ingredients of a vision of community typical for modernity.

An example of a social phenomena recalling a common religious identity and describing itself as a community of people of the same descent, understood as a part of a common cultural heritage, is a group of emancipatory movements of Afro-Americans in the United States. These movements present a quite colorful mix of the world's great religions (Islam and Christianity) as well genuine constructions of nativistic religious identities, appealing to an alleged common root of all black Americans. These movements, like the Nation of Islam, use the category of community in the meaning described above. Its basis is being made by an objectified concept of race, treated as a potential ingredient of identity. Not without reason within such movements people speak of the need to "wake up" an Afro-American spirituality or the need to stir up in this part of American society a feeling of pride of its own cultural and racial heritage.

From the beginning of the 1960s in the United States a process of the erosion of racial views and concepts had taken place, at least in the public discourse and the institutions of public life. Its culmination happened in 1968 when in the United States we could feel at that time the wind of revolutionary sentiments of counterculture, just like in the Old Continent. That year James Earl Ray had shot Martin Luther King, and black American athletes publicly expressed through a symbolic gesture their support for the Black Panthers organization during the Olympic games in Mexico. This decade of socio-cultural transgression had many dimensions, and one of the most important turned out to be the Afro-American movement. Its social influence was at that time slight, but two decades later it was supposed to be a beginning of a new social order – an order which clearly denied the existing relations between various social groups in the USA and pointed out the need for their radical redefinition.

At this time the actions of Afro-American organizations were intensified to work out a common level of identity. Afro-American political activists like Malcom X (born as Malcolm Little) had expressed more and more loudly the postulate of rejecting the existing ideological order, which was an expression of the oppressive domination of the "white man," and creating an ideologically attractive alternative for the self-identification of all those who were by this system humiliated and deprived of their basic civil rights. In the context of these years this was a very important postulate because of the fact that the issue of the legal status of black Americans became a basis for many emancipatory debates.

The roots of these debates lay upon the system of racial segregation legal in many states of USA. The process of the erosion of the legal barriers was possible due to the social activism of Afro-Americans, fighting for example for an equal access to education. One of the most fundamental decisions in this matter is related to the court case "Brown vs. Topeka Board of Education," which in 1954 had significantly moved the American society. It recognized the division of public schools due to racial differences of pupils as unconstitutional, and by doing so it had ended racial segregation in the American public life institutions, which had lasted since the end of 19th-century and had its origins in the famous "Plessy vs. Fergusson" case.[7] By the court's decision a view had been rejected, that said that the continuation of the politics of racial segregation was justifiable in public schools, based on alleged natural (racial) differences between the Afro-American pupils and the white majority. This view was to a large extent reflective of the imagination of racial dif-

[7] Casus „Plessy vs. Fergusson" from 1896 did point out the supreme character of state law over the federal law and sanctioned the principle "separate but equal" in the public life in the USA.

ferences valid in the American society in that time and simultaneously it objectified it as a given reality.

The Nation of Islam and its activists like Wallace D. Fard Muhammad and Louis Farrakhan expressed quite radical views on the character of necessary changes in the American society. With time, the slogans of Islamic organizations uniting black Americans were more and more close to a new segregationism, especially when they included in its rhetoric anti-Semitic, antigovernment, and anti-system ideas. The rejection of existing institutions, legal order, and the worldview framework typical for the white majority created an ideological vacuum, which had to be filled as quickly as possible. The Sunni Islam shared by the members of the Nation of Islam sometimes took a shape far from the doctrines known from the Middle East. This organization, especially Farrakhan, had popularized for a long time its own version of cosmology, in which the Earth and the Moon and all the continents were once close to Asia.

Not all Afro-Americans were willing to accept such a radical change. However, most of them did agree that the hitherto worldview was a product of a long lasting process of rooting out their "African identity" and replacing it with the ideas of the whites. The indigenous dimension of these slogans had also included the issue of spirituality. Christianity, so ardently practiced in the south of USA by many Afro-Americans, turned out to be just one more tool of domination. Christian institutional structures were insufficient to unite all Afro-Americans under the banners of the new liberation movement. One of the advocates of this view and a student of Malcolm X, was Maulana Karenga (born as Ronald McKinley Everett), the author of the idea of a new, purely Afro-American holiday named by him Kwanzaa.

Karenga's idea seemed to be brilliantly simple. In place of the old Christian holidays we have to bring to the fore their Afro-American counterparts. Kwanzaa was supposed to correspond to all the requirements of the new ideology of the revitalization of identities lost in the past. As the reference point, served the widely understood African culture. Therefore, Kwanzaa is a very syncretic religious holiday, based on content taken from many different African religions. The name of the holiday was taken from the Swahili language ("matunda ya kwanza" – the first fruit of the harvest), which functions in many parts of the African continent as a lingua franca. The universal character of the language was supposed to point out the unity of all black Americans, along the idea of a pan-Africanism. The holiday lasts for a week from the 26th of December to the 1st of January, and the first celebration of Kwanzaa took place in 1966.

In the center of the ideology behind this holiday lies "Nguza Saba," or "the seven principles of being black," that is "Umoja" (unity – the principle of family unity, local community, nation and race), "Kujichagulia" (self-determination – the principle of defining who we are, creation and self-expression), "Ujima" (collective work and responsibility – the principle of a collective solutions of problems by all members of the local community, mutual support and contribution to the community's existence), "Ujamaa" (collective economy – the principle of doing business together, from which profits are meant for the local community), "Nia" (goal – the principle of acting on the community's progress and bringing back to Afro-American culture its lost magnificence), "Kuumba" (creativity – the principle of acting with correspondence to create strength, acting the best we can and by doing so leaving future generations a better community) and "Imani" (faith – the principle of believing with our whole heart in family, other community members, teachers and leaders). To the ritual attributes of Kwanzaa belongs also a set of seven candles (each colour represents each principle of "Nguza Saba"), fruits and vegetables (a symbol of harvest and wealth), as well as characteristic clothing called "kente," stylized on traditional clothing from Central Africa.

In its ideological aspect Kwanzaa is, as Karenga states, an expression of a community spirit of the Afro-Americans and a specific "philosophy of community." Although the popularity of this holiday ended with the decrease in popularity of the Afro-American emancipation movements, today we may observe a phenomena of the inclusion of white Americans among the Kwanzaa followers. Even more, the holiday is celebrated in many public institutions in the USA, where Afro-Americans are a minority among the employees. The inclusion into the public life of the content brought by Kwanzaa and the movement gathered around Karenga is just a shadow of its past popularity, but it is worth mentioning that the American culture's mainstream is being joined today to marginal elements like Kwanzaa. Despite a significant drop in interest in this holiday among Afro-Americans, this suggests that a particularization of religious experience may result from the search for new, alternative towards the dominant order cultural identities alternative towards the dominant order, based not on objectified determinants, but purely worldview issues.

If we speak of modern religious movements, meaning the straightforward example of this mechanism, it is worth to look at the other pole, that is, those movements whose members constitute communities beyond the traditional barriers and in contrast to local communities. A deterritorialization of the religious experience is being realized fully in the sphere of the new media.

The global and, as it is defined, anti-authoritarian character of the Internet has caused a true explosion of religious movements, denominations and churches. The possibility of an unlimited expression of the need to define self-identification on the web generates new, sometimes peculiar, forms of religiosity. A perfect example of one apparently imagined world and purely constructivist doctrine is the identification of young people with religion based not in the real world, but in cinematographic fiction – the Jedi knights.

The movement of the followers of the Jedi knights religion has its roots in the movie saga by George Lucas's "Star Wars." The first signs of the new movement appeared in 2001, when the census in Australia, Canada and the United Kingdom revealed a surprising number of over half a million people who, under "confession," filled in their religious denomination as "Jedi." The movement itself is very diverse when it comes to denominations contributing to its appearance, but all of them do present a convergence in relation to their doctrine. The Jedi religion, just like the cinematographic original, does draw its roots from the religions of the Far East (Buddhism, Shinto, Hindu), Christianity, as well some philosophical and religious traditions of the West (gnosis). Nevertheless, Jediism is a relatively new phenomenon, and has little social influence. This does not change the fact that it presents an important tendency in the matter of new forms of religiosity. Jediism is supposed to be, according to some fans of the Lucas saga, an answer to the contemporary materialism, the race for success, and a life constantly on the move. Becoming a Jedi knight requires a lot of patience. The members of real world Jedi orders are joined by the symbols created in the movie (on the other hand, it is known that Lucas was inspired by the Japanese samurai codex) and are sensitive to all references to the cinematographic source. Especially the content that refers to an undefined "force" does cause a great interest among the movie fans. They create a community, whose members are bound together by a conviction of uniqueness of their identity. The identity constructed by these people is simultaneously a reconstruction of an imagined world. Complex rituals, the order's hierarchy and a sophisticated visual aspect do increase the number of followers of this fast growing religious phenomena. The community of the Jedi knights makes, however, a group that is characterized by a self-identification which puts in the center of its system of ideas a vision of a global community of people for whom religion is a strategy of dealing with reality without any axioms. It is a product of western cultural processes, as well pop-culture itself, which set the field for the identity building not just of the modern Jedi, but also many other religious formations.

Chapter 8

Preppers, EDC, and the new millenarianism

Henry David Thoreau, the American author, poet and philosopher, spent in the Appalachian wilderness exactly two years, two months and two days, severing ties with the outside world and "living by the labor of his hands only." While in the woods, he wrote his best-known novel or, to be more precise, philosophical treatise and memoirs. Drawing upon the personal experiences of its author, "Walden" is the epitome of transcendental philosophy, a powerful current in American culture at the beginning of the 19th-century. Also, the book espoused a philosophy that exerted a lasting appeal on Thoreau-like loners, eremites, and outsiders inhabiting the fringes of the steadily expanding American civilization. One can thus consider Thoreau a pioneer of the blatant and demonstrative dismissal of technological and cultural advancements brought about by nascent modernity. "Walden" openly exposes the fragility of the fibres that hold together the tissue of civilization, never shying away from repudiating the comforts that modern men have found increasingly difficult to do away with. In Thoreau's book, all the material essentials of the 19th-century life are discredited as a mere ornamentation of the prevailing morals and aesthetics of the time. Living alone for over two years in a cabin built by his own means on the shores of Walden Lake, Thoreau refused to comply with the values governing social life set out by American Protestantism.

This rebellion, however, may have somehow missed the point: Thoreau was subsequently hailed by many of his kin as the very paragon of the American pioneer, the epitome of the relentless struggle against the hardships of life, the very best that America has to offer. Furthermore, it was no one else but Thoreau who introduced to the mainstream of American civic discourse the idea of the man of the frontier: an individual striving to overpower nature but firmly attached to certain core values of the American culture. It's a recurrent theme in American culture, exploited, among others, by Henry Miller, and often regarded as representing American values at their purest. The ideas informing "Walden" were later destined to lend legitimacy to a peculiar socio-cultural phenomenon that emerged during the Cold War and times of the global threat of a nuclear demise. It brought together people who, much like Thoreau, declined to entrust their future and fate to the government, to external institutions, or simply to anyone outside the trusted circle of the local community.

The anti-establishmentarian roots of Preppers continue to underpin the identity of this peculiar subculture, which spreads not only across the USA, but also elsewhere, including Europe. However, it must be said that the movement's inspirations are purely American. American society, along with its specific cultural and historical background, is the pre-eminent example of the growing trend to fit the elements of the religious worldview into the technology-intensive system of values. Preppers join a long list of survivalist movements that emerged mid-century in reaction to the threat of global nuclear conflict and other disasters that could compromise the social, economic, or political order, or even wipe out the entire human race. However improbable it may seem today, these fears arrested the imagination of a good part of the American society in the 1950s. This omnipresent menace manifested itself variously, ranging from the political unsettlement caused by the Soviet Union and other countries of the Eastern Block, to a vague anxiety that elements foreign to American culture might infiltrate the American society. It was perhaps the latter that particularly spoke to the imagination of Americans: an invasion from the outside, the country taking a wrong turn, or the imposition of foreign rule were recurrent themes in the American popular culture in the 1950s, most notably in the cinema (and particularly sci-fi) movies. How vulnerable mid-century Americans were was demonstrated by Orson Welles in his famous radio broadcast about an alien invasion aired on the radio in 1938 – which caused widespread panic. America was to be defended by any means available and against any imaginable aggressor, extra-terrestrial or otherwise. One had to protect the American way of life – with its family values, local communities, and Protestant morals and ethics.

It is particularly the latter that informs the ideology of the contemporary Preppers, who often emphasise that the Protestant work ethic and belief in God is all one needs to survive any given calamity. Another religious theme underpinning the ideological convictions of American Preppers is millenarianism, espoused also by many American denominations, such as the Mormons. Millenarianism is fuelled by a deep belief that civilization and social order are in a state of severe crisis. According to Peppers, the world is on the verge of a great demise; consequently, the first and only task is to prepare thoroughly for the doomsday that is never far off. However, the end of the world preached by Preppers isn't envisaged as a single-scenario apocalypse: Armageddon comes in all shapes and sizes, having more in common with Hollywood action movies rather than the probable course of events. The most popular themes include disasters caused by a sudden and unexpected natural phenomenon (an asteroid or a comet hitting the Earth, loss of the planet's magnetic poles, raging tornados, a global pandemy, or eruption of a supervolcano), or man-made calamities (the sudden crash of the economic order, war or other armed conflict, decay of the state and anarchy, political destabilisation, global energy crisis, etc.). Many Preppers believe that the world is coming to its close and watch even for the subtlest signs heralding his or her version of the apocalypse.

The structure, sources, or content of the Preppers' worldviews may seem inconsistent and self-contradictory, but the Preppers themselves perceive them as defining features of the world's order (or disorder, for that matter) and of what will be left behind once it is gone. The Preppers' millenarianism comes to the fore in their centring of their daily routine and way of life around the end-of-the-world theme. Similarly to the Mormons, Preppers believe that only the well prepared will survive the forthcoming calamities. It's perhaps not without relevance that many Preppers interpret the world through popular myths of contemporary culture, for example oversimplified religious symbolism and numerology. One example for this is the year 2012 – when Preppers across the USA were galvanised into action following (popular scientific rather than purely scientific) revelations about the ancient Mayan calendar.[1] This non-Christian inspiration is hardly an isolated example. This is because institutional religion (especially Catholi-

[1] A similar mechanism could be observed in 2000 amid fears concerning the global crash of computer networks due to the malfunction of outdated data storage solutions ("Y2K Bug"). Many Preppers used millenarian rhetoric to justify at that time their heightened activity.

cism) is treated by Preppers with mistrust and often perceived as a sphere influenced by various non-religious institutions, such as governments and all sorts of interest groups. Deeply believing that an apocalypse is in the offing, Preppers are always ready to train in all kinds of skills and acquire knowledge that may come in handy in the event of the catastrophe. Their daily life is therefore filled with constant drills and challenges, with the smallest mistakes deeply analysed in order to avoid them during the actual "bug out" (evacuation to a safe spot) or "bug in" (to hole-up in a house turned into a self-sufficient fortress for months to come). Improvisation is rather uninvited, each detail is constantly rehearsed (such as the order of bug-out activities) until the Preppers master them – if not perfectly, then at least to a satisfactory degree that makes them feel as if they are in control.

"Be always prepared" is a natural motto not only for Preppers, but also those who, while not subscribing to the movement explicitly, show strikingly similar behaviour and share comparable worldviews. This is the case of a subculture called Everyday Carry (EDC). It associates individuals collecting items that may prove useful in case of any potentially deadly emergencies of daily life, such as accidents, blackouts, or floods. The list of items collected by EDC aficionados is quite extensive, but it always contains certain essentials. A typical EDC set consists of a knife, a flashlight, and a multi-purpose tool of some description or other. The owner either further expands his collection or upgrades the tools already at hand. Interestingly, the actual functionality of specific items is often of secondary importance: while choosing the particular tool, the future user will pay particular attention to the brand and how it is rated by the professionals. By "professionals" EDC followers mean not craftsmen, but rather members of the military, police, rescue services, or extreme athletes. Regarded as experts in survival techniques, they enjoy considerable authority among non-professionals who lack knowledge, skills, or the necessary physique to withhold adversities (due to, for example, morbid obesity plaguing modern America). In effect, their equipment is often nothing more than a fashionable gadget, an item potentially useful, but dysfunctional in the hands of its owners who could be better off possessing simpler objects better suited for their actual abilities. Naturally, this dysfunctionality of items collected by the followers of the EDC philosophy comes with their focus being on cultural rather than the material aspects of their collectibles. EDC has a growing presence, particularly in the virtual world, with the number of Internet forums dedicated to the topic on a steady rise. EDC websites are full of photos, called "pocket dumps," displaying collections of the EDC items carried daily by their users.

Preppers and EDC enthusiasts attach great value to their items and routines, which must work perfectly to minimalise the risk of failure. At stake is the life of their loved ones not to mention their own. The winners in the race for the best knife or source of potable water always earn the praise of their fellow survivalists. More importantly, however, escaping unscathed from the potentially upcoming disaster is what is considered to be a redemption of sorts, the ultimate victory, defined as sheer physical survival and preservation of the existing and familiar order; it's also a victory over the less fortunate "damned" who would perish in the catastrophe. The religious overtones in Prepper rhetoric are by no means exceptional. Disaster is often perceived in transcendental categories, applied also to purely mundane activities, such as gearing up of the house or assembly of the emergency kit. This is because all these actions are part of a bigger picture and lead up to the final test. The day of reckoning comes with the disintegration of social bonds and cultural norms, when the meticulously practiced skills are to be put to final use. The day the "Shit Hits the Fan" (SHTF) is highly anticipated as a foregone conclusion, even while yet causing anxiety and a sense of menace. This ambivalence associated with the apocalypse is reflected in the dense structure of the Preppers' worldview. The inner logic of the latter manifests itself in a peculiar social practice, illogical to those outside it, but perfectly coherent for the Preppers themselves. This relationship between the worldview and action is – if we are to believe Pierre Bourdieu – distinctive for any social *praxis* as "practice has a logic which is not that of logic."[2] Any attempt to question their doomsday-centric worldview prompts an immediate response and harsh critique aimed at sceptics. The latter, derogatorily referred to as "Polly" or "Polyanna," are seen as either a threat or as good-for-nothing in the face of disaster. Preppers themselves face a similar opinion, often perceived by the mainstream as persons suffering from personality disorders, psychosis, or, in extreme cases, as an element of a larger conservative movement linked with paramilitary organizations, such as various state militias or vigilance committees.

American survivalists can therefore be seen as a part of a broader phenomenon, loosely related to the neoconservative turn in American politics. At the beginning of the Cold War, however, survivalists were part of a more general social trend gaining momentum worldwide. At the time when threat seemed natural and permanent, both Western and Communist societies were always prepared for an immediate transition to the state of emergen-

[2] P. Bourdieu, *Practical Reason: on the theory of action*, Stanford 1998, p. 82.

cy, with the latter widely expected soon to become the new permanence. The collective fear psychosis, planted skilfully in American minds by the policymakers and mass culture, has left many people still believing in the imminent doomsday. Popular visions of the end of the world served up by pop culture started a life of their own, inhabiting the social consciousness as urban legends, spread by word of mouth but never verified. Apocalypse has crept into everyday life, somehow obscured by daily routines, but always looming in the background with its horrifying images. The cyclic crises of the post-war world were often used to vindicate catastrophic visions. Be it the Cuban missile crisis of 1961, the global energy crises of 1973 and 1979, or Katrina's landfall in 2005, in Pepper understanding they are signs that the world is on the brink of final disintegration and degeneration.

This scenario has also its Horsemen of the Apocalypse. The usual suspects are the politicians in Washington, liberals and democrats, new youth subcultures, immigrants, Muslims, and many other groups that "Real Americans" find disturbing. The shared flaw of these environments is that they don't subscribe to traditional American family values, refuse to integrate with local communities, or simply fail to fit into the Prepper vision of the post-apocalyptic society. One person exerting in this respect a strong influence on the movement is Kurt Saxon (born Donald Sisco), author of a series of survivalist books (the most popular being "Poor Man's James Bond"), and a far-right activist. Saxon, who in his life has belonged to many organizations, including the American Nazi Party, the Church of Scientology, and the Church of Satan, advocated radical measures to purge American society from troublemakers and other elements destabilising political and social order. He therefore found it perfectly justified and rational to use force against – and to physically eliminate – students protesting at the American universities in the late 1960s and early 1970s. For Saxon, the decline of modern America, and thus the whole of Western civilization, came as a natural result of the erosion of values that he seeks to preserve. While his worldview represents rather an extreme case of Prepper ideology, it still can't be said that the political and ideological attitudes of average Preppers are on the liberal side. Their conservatism becomes clear when one considers their flagship institutions, such as the *American Preppers Network* (APN), a nationwide collaboration platform for individuals openly subscribing to the Prepper movement.

Although not the only institutional body of Preppers, APN is a perfect example of how the movement works to legitimise its actions and ideological standpoint. A majority of American Preppers support the beliefs and the political agenda advanced by the organization, which serve as a platform for making national politics and introducing Prepper ideology to the public discourse in America. The strategy has worked: today the government recognizes the movement as a valid partner in the debate on national security. This stamp of approval has increased the movement's influence on specific emergency policies enforced by state legislatures and local communities. APN can thus be perceived as one of the platforms organizing local communities. This is even the more so considering that for APN the family is the fundamental unit of society and the essential element of mutual aid structures formed by Preppers. What is the APN's definition of a Prepper? According to its official website, "a Prepper is a person who takes Personal Responsibility and Self Reliance seriously." This rather vague phrasing is further unpacked in "The Five Principles of Preparedness" and the "Path of the Prepper" – walked by the Prepper to achieve excellence in preparedness. The Five Principles of Preparedness include: 1) Thrift and Frugality, 2) Seeking to be Independent, 3) Becoming Industrious, 4) Striving Towards Self Reliance, 5) Aspiring to have a year's supply of every needful thing.[3]

The Path of the Prepper introduces a simple five-stage instruction to acquire the necessary skills and to increase the numbers of followers.[4] It is initiated by phase one, in which one explores preparedness and becomes aware of potential dangers with all their inevitability. The candidate is thus encouraged to ask questions and learn specific skills by following the example of "Mentors," individuals experienced in survivalist techniques. Next comes phase two, where candidates practice new skills collectively to achieve perfection (often via blogs, online videos, Internet forums). Phase three consists in an accommodation of new skills to one's life by sharing resources and technical skills. In phase four, Preppers choose one skill and become experts in the given area (e.g. energy supply, communication, firearms or steel weapons, hunting, medicine, etc.). During the fifth and last phase, Preppers practice their skills of choice and become mentors to others, both in the practical and the ideological sphere.

The religious analogies of the above set of rules and principles are all too obvious. They are firmly rooted in and promote the Protestant work

[3] http://americanpreppersnetwork.com/the-five-principles-of-preparedness [date of entry: 23.10.2013].

[4] http://americanpreppersnetwork.com/path-of-the-prepper [date of entry: 23.10. 2013].

ethic and the principles of social life studied by Max Weber. For example, Prepper specialisation in just one survivalist area (one in which one excels) can be analysed in terms of the Weberian category of vocation. The American Protestantism and Puritan overtones present in Prepper ideology can be further framed into a bigger picture of the consumerist model evolving today in the American culture. Hard work, although rather physical than intellectual, self-reliance fuelled by disregard for the powers and supremacy of the state, strict moral and ethical values, accumulation of (other than financial) capital – all these elements strongly define the Prepper worldview and play a vital role in justifying their social practice. This relationship between ideology and social *praxis* has also its symbolic dimension, in which these core values are translated into material categories, now devoid of their primary meaning. Be it compulsive shopping for increasingly expensive and technologically advanced tools used by EDC enthusiasts or for lavish supplies of food and essential goods kept at home by Preppers, both phenomena testify to the hyperconsumerism pervading the American society. Neither the EDC items nor Preppers' supplies will ever be properly utilised, however, because post-capitalist society destroys their primary purpose: consumption is no longer the key reason for purchase, which now serves to satisfy artificial needs and maintain a certain standard of living.

The American-style consumerism duly represented by Preppers and EDC testifies to a society that embraces purchases and material possessions as its core values. A good Prepper always has solid supplies and can anytime manifest his or her individualism by switching to a self-preservation mode. A good consumer possesses desirable products and puts his or her exceptional lifestyle on full display. These models are not mutually exclusive, but complement each other. The consumerist analogy is applicable to both the Preppers and EDC – it just relates to a different catalogue of products. A knife or a flashlight can save one's life only when provided by a recognized brand.[5] The consumer society values demonstrative and public consumption, and survivalists are no exception to this rule.

The aforementioned "pocket dump" vividly resembles the religious practices of the indigenous Americans, notably the potlatch. During the pot-

[5] It would seem that EDC enthusiasts use a wide variety of products. As a matter of fact their stamp of approval is given only to a very limited number of brands perceived as reliable (e.g. Surefire flashlights, Spyderco penknives, Magpul firearms accessories, or Tad Gear clothes). Their symbolic value carries also a very tangible value as they're often also very costly, even by American standards.

latch ceremony, North American Indians engaged in the public destruction of valued items (blankets, pottery, etc.). The proceedings determined the social status of the participants, with respect and prestige being proportional to the number and value of possessions one was willing to sacrifice. "Pocket dump" is a symbolic potlatch of cyber culture. Carefully arranged pictures represent aesthetic and symbolic value. They are posted online and use a visual language easily grasped by the followers of EDC websites. Much like in potlatch, where each detail of the ritual is rigorously predefined, the composition of a "pocket dump" picture and its reception among Internet users are highly ritualized, with comments on more interesting collections emphasising their meanings and communicative value, not their potential use.

Items define their users and Internet commentators in a chaotic world full of incomprehensible cultural phenomena and disquieting natural anomalies – hence the omnipresent metaphor of apocalypse, which EDC enthusiasts and Preppers understand as the ultimate test for their value as human beings. To survive the apocalypse, or just about any calamity or accident, is to assert the supremacy of man and civilization over nature, and its unpredictable character. The Preppers' dreams of the simple life, governed by traditional values, are therefore self-contradictory. On this account, man is conceived as a creature incapable of independent existence, reliant on civilizational skills and technology. A knife or a flashlight become a cultural extension of bodily functions, indispensable to handle even the simplest routines. We are being therefore forced to amass compulsively various goods and specialists tools. Simultaneously this very consumption is being postponed in terms of physical features of consumption and turns into a more metaphorical vision of what is available to us for consumption. The acquisition of those goods is more important than their use itself, with related knowledge and expertise somehow blurred and vague. These skills seem to come with meanings attached to the items, rather than as a result of the actual practice and effort. To quote Jean Baudrillard: "Consumer goods thus present themselves as *harnessing of power*, not as products embodying work."[6]

---

[6] J. Baudrillard, *The Consumer Society: Myths and Structures*, London 1998, p. 32.

Chapter 9

A pearl in the crown. Concerning Banksy

The British Empire had its greatest moments of glory when continental Europe was lost in a chaos of various folk revolutions, power wars and the period of the economic and ideological destabilisation that was present on the eve of the Great War between European nations. However, the British crown took care to make the imperial creation "on which the sun never sets" function efficiently, and to effectively multiply the capital, both financial and cultural, that had been invested in it. The symbolic expressions of the colonial domination of British culture deeply infiltrated those corners of the world where the influence of the Crown was clearly visible, as well as those in which the presence of the stewards of Queen Victoria was less obvious. Notwithstanding this, the British model of thinking about the world has become one of the most important elements of the Western civilisation paradigm for a long long time. That paradigm, carried together with the area of actual political domination of the West spreading with dizzy speed, has established the conviction of the invariability of Pax Britannica for many years. The world order structured in such a way brought both the blessing of the industrial revolution and social conflicts alike, which were growing together with the structural stratification observable between the bourgeoisie and the working class. At the turn of the 19th and 20th-century, Britain was a place which the interest of the world focused on. The performance of the London stock exchange decided on the lot of a considerable part of the inhabitants of the Old Continent, and the colonial dominions and the regions where the English language was prevalent were supposed to form the borders of the Western civilisation.

At that time, it was undoubtedly India that formed the greatest pearl in the British Crown. The interest in the Orient expressed by the British manifested itself not only in particularist political actions in Asia, but also in a fascination with Oriental aesthetics and cultural motifs that was difficult to explain. Both the British and European painting, architecture and literature of the 19th-century quickly seized on the strands related to the East, which were interpreted as the quintessence of exoticism. Towards the end of the 19th-century, India with its magnetic charm attracted brawlers, artists and people avid for fame and a career of all sorts.. In his novels, Rudyard Kipling grasped perfectly well the *Zeitgeist* of this age, full of peculiar enthusiasm. His "Kim" presents the way in which the British of the time pursued their vision of the rule of "divide and rule" in a vivid manner. It was not uncommon of them to employ a directly authoritarian regime and the administrative structures related to it in establishing a new order in India, an order which was based on the conviction that it is possible to build an idealised society from scratch and to make it a reflection of the British society, with the only difference being its lack of historical conditioning. The image of that society was reflected not only in Kipling's "Kim," but also in a considerable part of the art and literature of the time. The Orient seemed to be omnipresent, both through strands related to the Far East and the intense interest in Egypt. Not only did the ancient cultures of the East provide aesthetic inspirations, but they also suggested that the fossilised British customs could gather a new momentum owing to the incorporation of Eastern exoticism. It was the first time that the rigid structure of the British society at the turn of the 19th and 20th-century was subject to a peculiar contestation pursued by the new generation of intellectuals, artists and outstanding personalities of the world of culture, such as Arthur Conan Doyle or Oscar Wilde. Thus, the fascination with the Orient mentioned above became an immanent part of the British culture of that period, both in terms of ideology and through the presence of Oriental strands in the public space (mainly in architectural styles). Respectable British cultural institutions, such as the *British Museum*, for instance, quickly seized on the new fashion. The museums and galleries in London started to be filled with exhibits which had to relate to the intellectual demand for the Orient in one way or another out of necessity. The popularity of this phenomenon surpassed the wildest dreams. In every self-respecting *high society* house in London there were objects from and references to the cultures of the East.

At this point, however, it has to be noted that the fashion for the Orient at the time involved a relatively narrow section of the British society – the one that stood on the threshold of modernity. Broad social masses, deprived of any direct influence on the shape of the mainstream of British culture, not so much interested in seeking cultural inspirations, but rather created a culture which was peculiar in terms of its quality and independent from the *upper class* – a culture that was later to become the stirring of contemporary popular culture. Simultaneously with the British Orientalism of the late Victorian age, the culture of the working class developed, constituting a peculiar reversal of the ideas standing behind the life strategies of the British bourgeoisie and aristocracy. The stratification of the interests of particular social strata, which became visible as early as in the second half of the 19th-century, became reflected in the phenomena of a cultural nature as well in the next years. In some cases, the otherness of the new customs pursued by the working class, as well as the affluent middle and upper class, was emphasised in a radical manner in both social practice and communication. The sense of exclusion from the mainstream of life, observable among the representatives of the lower strata of the British society, has constituted an important part of the social discourse in Britain since the beginning of the 20th-century. The result of these frictions was the emergence of the mass culture phenomenon, which shaped today's popular culture to a considerable extent in the opinion of many researchers. The aesthetic preferences of the English working class obviously contested the upper culture of the British society, although in the majority of cases it was an unintentional expression of social dissatisfaction with their position they occupied in the social structure.

As far as the social level is concerned, the processes taking place in Britain in the 20th-century involved the existing social structure to a large extent. Durkheim's statement concerning the manifestations of that structure in all phenomena of human life seemed to find its confirmation at that stage. Notwithstanding this, the processes of modernisation that came along with the age of modernity also involved the problem of the structural diversity of social groups in the United Kingdom. In this regard, the turning point of World War II constituted one of the most important constituents of the debate on the present shape of British popular culture. This was because the post-war London became a place where one could observe social and cultural transformations taking place in a rapid manner, which were quite important not only for the whole of such a rigidly established British system of values, but also for a considerable part of the paradigm of Western civilisation. At the beginning of the 1950s, not only did the British juvenile scene, existing next to the strongly political French juvenile culture of the time, inscribe itself perfectly well in the emerging trend of counterculture, but it also influenced it in a creative manner through new trends in music, visual arts, literature, film, or fashion. The "English style" was *de facto* one of the most popular ones, drawing inspiration from tradition and setting new aesthetic challenges, as well as creating new conceptual forms that were distant from the accepted standards.

The 1960s in Britain were both a period of fast economic growth and a contestation of the existing social order. Broad-based social projects kept rapidly changing both the British landscape and the mentality of the new generation alike. Old symbols gained new meaning, with new subject references being ascribed to them. London was to become a city that would live in step with the new rhythm, marked by hippie ideals on the one hand and the peculiarly British context around the processes of change at that time on the other. The *swinging London* – that was how the atmosphere of the city was defined then – was a true Mecca for various kinds of artistic personages, media celebrities and people hungry for the big-city fame. The very notion of a "swinging London" became popular mainly due to the media in London, seeking some catchy slogan that could grasp the nature of the atmosphere in this city in the 1960s. Apart from Liverpool, London had all the attributes of what fell under the term "cool," in the case of which the range of notional references was widening in proportion to the number of juvenile music bands and well-known figures of the British media at the time, e.g. the model Twiggy or the famous representatives of the British artistic scene, such as the painters Peter Blake, David Hockney or Victor Pasmore. The Beatles, The Rolling Stones, The Who and many other music bands unquestionably set the trend for the London turmoil, and the images of British pop-art defined aesthetic limits to a large extent. The vitality of the city was grasped in a perfect manner by the Italian director Michelangelo Antonioni in the film entitled "Blow-Up" – one of the most representative film images related to the 1960s. In this film, we can observe a condensed representation of the ideals of the English generation of the age of Mini Coopers, London clubs and the subculture of the Mods. However, the significance of the film allows no space for doubts as to the place of an individual in a world so deeply infiltrated by cultural symbols. In the final scene of the film, the main protagonist surrenders to a dancing crowd of young people, abandoning any attempts to step beyond the accepted conventions. As John Fiske points out, he ultimately internalises what until recently meant the hegemonic reign of the imperatives of pop-culture, for he only tolerates only those of the contestation movements that inscribe their rebellion in the slogans of a generational uprising. As far as the system is concerned, however, they are not a centrifugal trend, but a factor that consolidates and integrates pop-societies. Thus, the generational change did not entail any deep social consequences, at least as far as the structural ordering of British culture is concerned. It was still possible to observe an interfusion of content and strands between the strongly hierarchical classes of the British society. This time, however, such mobility did not encounter any institutional barriers. Moreover, it was not uncommon for the English *high society* to boast of having contacts with the world of the new British music and artistic scene, as well as with the new television celebrities.

As I have already pointed out, popular culture in the Britain of the 1960s shaped the attitudes of young people not only through its slogans of contestation, but also owing to the influence of new aesthetic forms[1]. Traditional British art was based on figurative representations of reality. It comes as no surprise, then, that the paintings created by such artists as Francis Bacon fuelled controversy and confusion in the world of art on the British Isles. However, insofar as Bacon's paintings were interpreted as an expression of a nonconformist process of artistic creation, both the trend set by Bacon and the other similar trends of British painting clearly referred, although through an inversion, to such authors as Edward Turner, as well as to the painting traditions of the 19th-century. Bacon's popularity also translated into financial success and secured a prominent position for him both in the history of art and among the British establishment. This type of significant relation between the British world of art and the particularist social conditions was to be observed in the next decades as well. Admittedly, it was not appurtenant to the unique British or English character exclusively. However, it is this area where it has gained specific expression in recent years. Adaptation of the ideology of protest and Nonconformity by institutions that symbolise an exact opposition of these attitudes became a typical mechanism of the social digestion of those trends in art that undermined the existing order.

Together with the beginning of the 1990s, the British style was nothing more than a memory. The sense of emptiness in the popular culture of the post-Thatcher age shared by the young people translated into the language

[1] See S. Levy, *Ready, Steady, Go!: The Smashing Rise and Giddy Fall of Swinging London*, London 2003.

of cultural and aesthetic references present in the media. The rave culture and the so-called new dance scene kept gaining increasing popularity in Britain. The trance rhythms of electronic music did not bring any new postulates, they were not politically marked and did not demand anything more than one thing – a never-ending hedonistic dancing trance. Simultaneously with the development of the rave scene and political reshuffles, British pop music experienced a sudden invigoration. The term "Cool Britannia" began its brilliant career in the media, constituting an obvious paraphrase of the patriotic chant "Rule Britannia." The revival of the image of the country was intended to mean its rejuvenation, in the political sense as well. Tony Blair's government, which replaced Margaret Thatcher's cabinet, was to embody the new British extravagance. The etymology of the very term derives from the 1960s, where it appeared in one of the songs by the *Bonzo Dog Doo Dah Band*. Other sources claim that the term was borrowed from the kind of popular ice-cream sold under the name of *Ben & Jerry's*, allegedly symbolising the taste of Britain. The slogan anyhow was quickly adopted by the media and became popular owing to such events as placing it on the cover of the *Newsweek* magazine, for instance. Of course, attentive observers did not miss the remark that the phrase "Cool Britannia" also referred to the popularity of the term "swinging London" and was understood as an unrefined pastiche of the latter. In the middle of 1990s, however, it made a stay for good in both the public space and in the media, also owing to the fact of ascribing to this phenomenon a certain section of the British music scene, collectively referred to as brit-pop. The following bands can be included in the brit-pop of that trend: Oasis, Blur, Elastica, Pulp, The Verve, and several others. A few years later, the outburst of popularity of the term made visible the attempts of its semantic transfer into the local context of particular countries of the *Commonwealth* (*Cool Cymru*, *Cool Caledonia*). A farewell to this notion eventually took place at the moment in which the Labourite Prime Minister Tony Blair, unequivocally identified with that term, retired from his post.

At that time, the British artistic scene also remained in a kind of a standstill, in spite of the emergence of important initiatives, such as the opening of the Tate Gallery and the creation of the artistic enclave in the neighbourhood of the London Docks from scratch. However, both London and the British artistic world still kept searching for its own identity. Formal experiments and the employment of shock, as was the case with Sarah Kane's plays, seemed to be in the long run merely secondary remakes of well-tried motifs. In the nearby city of Bristol, a group of artists and musicians developed in a certain opposition to the London scene, offering a slightly different perspective on the shape of popular culture in the country. Towards the end of the 1990s, such bands as Portishead, Massive Attack or the artist known as Tricky set the framework of the music trend called trip-hop. This trend combined vocal techniques appurtenant to hip-hop music with an original message, sometimes even a shocking artistic entourage, and a universalistic significance of lyrics that alternately touched upon the problems of everyday life and important life issues instead of generational dilemmas. Together with the emergence of trip-hop, a rapid development of the art of graffiti in Bristol also became noticeable. Drawings and murals began to appear on the streets of the city, but the use of a stencil technique was somewhat of a novelty. This technique, consisting in creating relatively simple images in terms of their form, amazed the inhabitants of the city with their apt observations of a social and political nature. The artists from Bristol drew their inspiration from the New York art, which came into an artistic dialogue with the public space in an equally uncompromising manner.

Some of the most interesting graffiti works were the ones signed with the mysterious alias "Banksy." As it soon turned out, Banksy's works gained a status of cult creations among the young people of Bristol. However, that enthusiasm was not shared by some group of inhabitants of the city, who accused Banksy of ordinary vandalism. In spite of the growing popularity of the artist and his works, some voices could be heard indicating that the increase in the interest in street art created by Banksy implied direct economic consequences for the local community. This was because Banksy received the following e-mail signed with the name Daniel:

"I don't know who you are or how many of you there are but I am writing to ask you to stop painting your things where we live. In particular xxxxxx road in Hackney. My brother and me were born here and have lived here all our lives but these days so many yuppies and students are moving here neither of us can afford to buy a house where we grew up anymore. Your graffities are undoubtably part of what makes these wankers think our area is cool. You're obviously not from round here and after youve driven up the house prices youll probably just move on. Do us all a favour and go do your stuff somewhere else like Brixton."[2]

---

[2] Original spelling maintained. *Banksy. Wall and Piece*, London 2006, p. 130.

However, it was difficult to name the offender. The mysteriousness and anonymity of the artist, carefully structured in the media, became legendary.[3] Admittedly, there were some snippets of information in the British press on the decipherment of the artist's identity from time to time, but it soon turned out that it was nothing more than a deliberate act of information sabotage that he had prepared himself. The media also became part of his artistic *entourage*. As the *Daily Mail* reports, the most plausible sources indicated that the real name of the artist disguised under the alias Banksy is Robert (or Robin or Robden) Gunningham. Another version indicates the name of Robert Banks. It is obvious that Banksy is perfectly aware of the role the media play today in the process of artistic creation, particularly the one that enters into the realm of social discourse, politics and dialogue with conventions and cultural tradition. The most famous example of this latter approach is the pictorial paraphrase of the well-known painting by Edward Hopper – *Nighthawks*. It seems the version created by Banksy contains all the familiar elements of the original. Taking a closer look at the composition of the painting, however, we can clearly observe that instead of a person looking through the window at people sitting inside a night-club, we find an archetypal representation of the British representative of the working class, who is throwing a brick into the window. The problem of the degradation of culture marked in this work is more than clear for the majority of contemporary British people. We can identify the figure in the painting with the phenomenon of the mass tourism pursued by many British people from the lower stratas of the society, which is far from the standard customs accepted on the British Isles. The symbolic vandalism depicted in the painting is actual vandalism. However, it is not pursued by the author himself, but by the viewer who ignores the meaning of the original work by Hopper being paraphrased. Thus, the intellectual void of British reality is filled with the taste of the masses.

The conceptual intention presented above co-creates one of the most important trends in Banksy's work. The use of black, albeit simultaneously extremely apt, humour is also not unfamiliar to him. In order to pursue this intention, Banksy often does not stop short of doing an artistic provocation, simultaneously making a funny performance. In 2004 and 2005, for instance, he planted copies of classic paintings in well-known European and American

[3] C. Laureen, "Banksy was here. The invisible man of graffiti art," *The New Yorker*, 14.05.2007.

museums. However, his versions of the paintings contained some elements that were significantly different from the originals. The copy of Mona Lisa prepared by Banksy and planted in the Louvre in Paris in 2004, had the commonly recognised sign known as the so-called *smiley* instead of the face of La Gioconda. Another provocation, done in the Brooklyn Museum in 2005, was slightly more subtle. The figure of a typical 18th-century English nobleman presented in the painting was surrounded by signs derived from contemporary graffiti and the nobleman himself held a can of spray paint. What is interesting, that work was not removed earlier than after eight days, which was when the museum staff finally noticed a painting that did not actually constitute part of the exhibition. No one of the visitors recognised the forgery, regarding it as an authentic element of the museum's composition. There are plenty of similar examples, not to mention the famous forgery of an archaeological artefact, which in Banksy's version presented a gatherer-hunter hunting bison with a shopping trolley. The work was accompanied by an appropriate note below it which stated that it was a "[...] finely preserved example of primitive art dates from the Post-Catatonic era, [...] under the moniker Banksymus Maximus but little else is known about him. Most of this type has unfortunately not survived. The majority is destroyed by zealous municipal officials who fail to recognise the artistic merit and historical value of daubing on walls."[4] However, the witty remark Banksy smuggled into this short text is essentially related to the deep conviction of his that the systemic solutions utilised by state institutions are inadequate for the living fabric of city life.

This thesis finds its ground in the critique of the policy employed by the authorities of many British cities towards all forms of vandalism, including graffiti. In Banksy's opinion, the so-called theory of "broken windows" has clearly failed along the whole line and its practical applications constitute merely another step towards the dehumanisation of urban space. This theory, being a theoretical model from the field of criminology, was presented by James Q. Wilson and George L. Killing in 1982 in the famous article entitled "Broken Windows."[5] According to this theory, constant monitoring of urban space in order to prevent acts of vandalism is also intended to minimise the possibility of a spreading social disorder and the occurrence of more serious crimes. In the opinion of Wilson and Killing, the factors supposed to prevent

[4] *Banksy. Wall...*, p. 185.

[5] http://www.theatlantic.com/magazine/archive/1982/03/broken-windows/304465/ [20.12.13].

these phenomena from occurring are to be the influence of social norms and conformist attitudes, the presence of mechanisms of monitoring and signalling unlawful actions, as well as the social awareness of the inevitability of sanctions related to the commitment of an offence or crime. This theory has found reflection in the policy pursued by the municipal authorities of New York towards the end of 1990s, when the city was governed by Mayor Rudolph Giuliani. However, the effectiveness of this kind of reasoning was subject to broad-based criticism, for it did not take into consideration the influence of many other factors, such as the dynamics of social change.[6]

In this regard, the motifs of omnipresent closed circuit television that Banksy employs in his art in the form of the figures of policemen and soldiers, indicate a strong political verve of the British artist. For him, the politicisation of urban space has become a *fait accompli* we all have to face, transforming the existing barriers into a tool for expressing our own convictions. An excellent example of this is the series of graffiti images that Banksy put in 2005 on the concrete wall erected by the Israeli authorities to separate the West Bank of Jordan from the territory of Israel. These images suggest both the absurdity of the very idea, as well as the creative potential indwelling people. The motif of the future change of the social and political *status quo* visible in this project has also been present in his other works, particularly in the series of graffiti marked with the recurrent topic of rats and monkeys that symbolise bottom-up actions towards the change of the centres of power. In this case, the image of a chimpanzee holding a transparency with the slogan "Laugh now, but one day I'll be in charge" is symptomatic. Banksy himself perceives even an attempt to seize urban space by architectural forms that are unfriendly to humans as an attempt to mechanise and instrumentalise city life. Let me provide here the example of an inscription made using pink paint and a fire extinguisher on one of the buildings in Southbank in London in 2004, containing the slogan "Boring". Banksy took the raw form of concrete walls without windows, surrounded by other concrete office buildings, as an invitation, as well as a gauntlet thrown down to the artist. The same applies to the work which Banksy created in response to the action pursued by London authorities against urban graffiti. In 2006, Banksy placed an emergency telephone number, otherwise known to Londoners, under which any complaints about the emerging graffiti works could be reported,

---

[6] At this point, it is worth mentioning the critical studies in the field of criminology, created by David Thatcher.

on one of the walls at Pentonville Road. In his version, the inscription was being painted over by a boy equipped with a paintbrush and a bucketful of pink paint. The situation was similar also in the case of a graffiti placed on one of the buildings in London's Hackney in 2003. In this case, however, Banksy used the commonly-known scene from the film *Pulp Fiction* directed by Quentin Tarantino, where the main protagonists hold bananas in their hands instead of guns. This graffiti became one of distinctive features of Banksy's work. After some time, this graffiti was covered by another one, created by an unknown author. Two years later, however, Banksy returned to this place, creating a new work that constituted a peculiar paraphrase of the first one. This time, the shot depicted the two protagonists holding guns in their hands, but it was them who were transformed into bananas instead. The irony present in this graffiti concerns first of all Banksy himself, who, being aware of his increasing popularity, decided to mock both the authorities (this place is surrounded by police cameras) and himself at the same time.

Popular culture and its myths as such, also constitute the topic of artistic provocation in Banksy's work. In 2006, the artist replaced 500 copies of albums by Paris Hilton in music stores and the false ones were sold to clients in the number of several dozens before the staff noticed Banksy's provocation. It is startling that such an artistic provocation was met with an enthusiastic reception on the art market. The few existing copies of albums modified by Banksy that are available are still being successfully sold during art auctions today. After all, the commercial success of many of Banksy's works is typical for the British world of art in recent years. The most expensive of his works was sold in 2007 for an amount of over 100 thousand pounds on an auction held in the well-known Sotheby's auction house. Another issue is the so-called "Banksy's Effect" being openly discussed at present. It denotes a peculiar fashion of having either an original work by Banksy, or one of numerous reproductions of well-known graphical themes taken from his works, placed on typical gadgets of pop-culture, such as T-shirts or coffee mugs.

The "Banksy's Effect" observed today is an acute reminiscence of the frantic pursuit of the swinging spirit of London in the 1960s, as well as the trend towards Oriental souvenirs and the art of the second half of the 19th-century. However, insofar as the British Orientalism was typical of some specific groups of the British society and the "swinging London" was a city of ceaseless rock-and-roll carnival, the present admiration of the art of graffiti seems to be a phenomenon that singles itself out against the aforementioned phenomena in terms of both its disturbing the rules of artistic convention and its reversing the poles of the social reception of this form of art. The art of graffiti, until recently commonly deemed an act of vandalism (similarly as the whole of *street art*), has gained the favour of the decision-makers, is purchased by financial elites and treated as a capital investment. Sometimes, it is even promoted as an initiative, the purpose of which is to renew certain areas of urban space. Seen from this perspective, however, the figure of Banksy stands out with an artfully conducted game with artistic conventions and the social context related to them. As a result, the directions of artistic auto-creation that he follows are marked with an ironic attitude not only towards high culture or pop-culture, but also towards culture *per se* as such.

Bibliography

Anderson B., *Imagined Communities. Reflections on the Origin and Spread of Nationalism*, New Left Books, New York – London 2006.

Banks J. A., McGee Banks C., *Multicultural Education: Issues and Perspectives*, John Wiley & Sons Inc., Hoboken 2012.

Banksy. Wall and Piece, Random House UK, London 2006.

Baudrillard J., *The Consumer Society: Myths and Structures*, SAGE Publications Ltd., London 1998.

Bell D., *The Cultural Contradictions of Capitalism*, Basic Books, New York 2008.

Bennet D. (ed.), *Multicultural states: Rethinking difference and identity*, Routledge, London and New York 1998.

Boon J., *Other tribes, other scribes. Symbolic anthropology in the comparative study of cultures, histories, religions, and texts*, Cambridge 1982.

Bourdieu P., *Practical Reason: on the theory of action*, Stanford University Press, Stanford 1998.

Canet R., Pech L., Stewart M., "France's Burning Issue: Understanding the Urban Riots of November 2005," in forthcoming B. Bowden, M. David (eds.), *Riot: Resistance and Rebellion in Britain and France. 1381 to the Present*, 2013.

Chene M. des, "Symbolic Anthropology," in D. Levinson, M. Ember (eds.), *Encyclopedia of Cultural Anthropology*, Henry Holt & Co., New York 1996.

Clifford J., "Power and Dialogue in Ethnography. Marcel Griaule's Initiation," in G. W. Stocking Jr. (ed.), *Observers Observed. Essays on Ethnographic Fieldwork*, The University of Wisconsin Press, Madison & London 1983.

Clifford J., *The Predicament of Culture: Twentieth-Century Ethnography, Literature, and Art*, Harvard University Press, Cambridge 1988.

Cogley R. W., *John Eliot's mission before King Philip's War*, Harvard University Press, Harvard 1999.

Collins L., "Banksy was here. The invisible man of graffiti art," *The New Yorker*, 14.05.2007.

Deflem M., "Ritual, Anti-Structure, and Religion: A Discussion of Victor Turner's Processual Symbolic Analysis," *Journal for the Scientific Study of Religion*, 30 (1)/1991, pp. 1–25.

Dolgin J., Kemnitzer D. S., Schneider D. M. (eds.), *Symbolic Anthropology. A Reader in the Study of Symbols and Meanings*, Columbia University Press, New York 1977.

Douglas M., *Purity and Danger. An Analysis of Concepts of Pollution and Taboo*, A Butterworth-Heinemann Title, London and New York 2002.

Fallaci O., *The rage and the pride*, Rizzoli, New York 2002.

Fardon R., *Mary Douglas: An Intellectual Biography*, Routledge, London and New York 1999.

Fear-Segal J., "Nineteenth-Century Indian Education: Universalism Versus Evolutionism," *Journal of American Studies* 33/1999.

Feinberg W., *Common Schools/Uncommon Identities: National Unity and Cultural Difference*, Yale University Press, New Haven 2000.

Firth R., *Symbols. Private and Public*, George Allen & Unwin, London 1973.

Fischer E. F., McKenna-Brown R. (ed.), *Maya Cultural Activism in Guatemala*, University of Texas Press, Austin 1996.

Frazer J. G., *The golden bough. The study in magic and religion*, Palgrave, New York 2002.

Fuentes C., *A New Time for Mexico*, Farrar, Straus and Giroux, Berkeley and Los Angeles 1997.

Geertz C., *From the Native's Point of View. On the Nature of Anthropological Understanding*, in idem, *Local Knowledge. Further essays within the scope of interpretive anthropology*, Basic Books, New York 2000.

Geertz C., "School Building: A Retrospective Preface," in J. W. Scott, D. Keates (eds.), *Schools of Thought. Twenty-Five Years of Intepretative Social Science*, Princeton University Press, Princeton and Oxford 2001.

Geertz C., "Thick Description: Toward an Interpretive Theory of Culture," in idem, *The Interpretation of Cultures*, Basic Books, New York 1973.

Gellner E., *Postmodernism, Reason and Religion*, Routledge, London & New York 1992.

Giddens A., *The Consequences of Modernity*, Polity Press, Cambridge 1990.

Hansen J. F., *Sociocultural Perspectives on Human Learning: Foundations of Educational Anthropology*, Waveland Press Inc., Prospect Heights 1979.

Kennedy M. H., "Introduction," in E. S. Curtis, *The Plains Indian. Photographs of Edward S. Curtis*, The University of Nebraska Press, Lincoln 2001.

Levinson B. A., Foley D. E., Holland D. C. (eds.), *The Cultural Production of the Educated Person: Critical Ethnographies of Schooling and Local Practice*, State University of New York Press, Albany 1996.

Levy S., *Ready, Steady, Go!: The Smashing Rise and Giddy Fall of Swinging London*, Broadway Books, London 2003.

McKenna-Brown R., "The Mayan Language Loyalty Movement in Guatemala," in E. F. Fischer, R. McKenna-Brown (ed.), *Maya Cultural Activism in Guatemala*, University of Texas Press, Austin 1996.

Moore H. L. (ed.), *The Future of Anthropological Knowledge*, Routledge, London and New York 1996.

Ortner S., "Theory in Anthropology since the Sixties," in N. B. Dirks, G. Eley, S. Ortner (eds.) *Culture/Power/History. A Reader in Contemporary Social Theory*, Princeton University Press, Princeton 1993.

Peacock J. L., *The Anthropological Lens. Harsh Light, Soft Focus*, Cambridge University Press, Cambridge 2001.

Rabinow P., Sullivan W. M., "Interpretative Turn. A Second Look," in P. Rabinow, W. M. Sullivan (eds.), *Interpretative Social Science. A Second Look,* University of California Press, Berkeley and Los Angeles 1988.

Roberts J. I., Akinsanya S. K. (eds.), *Educational Patterns and Cultural Configurations: The Anthropology of Education*, David McKay Company Inc., New York 1976.

Said E., *Orientalism. Western Conceptions of the Orient*, Penguin Books, London 1995.

Schneider D. M., *American Kinship. A Cultural Account*, University of Chicago Press, Chicago and London 1980.

Schneider D. M., "Notes Toward a Theory of Culture," in K. Basso, H. A. Shelby (ed.), *Meaning in Anthropology*, University of New Mexico Press, Albuquerque 1976.

Shweder R. A., Good B. (ed.), *Clifford Geertz by his colleagues*, The University of Chicago Press, Chicago and London 2005.

Sperber D., *On Anthropological Knowledge. Three Essays*, Cambridge University Press, Cambridge 1987.

Spindler G. D. (ed.), *Doing the ethnography of schooling: Educational anthropology in action*, Waveland Press Inc., Long Grove 1982.

Spindler G. D. (ed.), *Education and Cultural Process: Anthropological Approaches*, Waveland Press Inc., Long Grove 1997.

Spindler G. D., *Education and Culture: Anthropological Approaches*, Holt, Rinehart, and Winston, New York, Chicago, San Francisco, Toronto and London 1963.

Stocking Jr. G. W., *Victorian Anthropology*, The Free Press, New York 1987.

Tibi B., *Fundamentalizm religijny*, PIW, Warsaw 1997.

Trafzer C. F., Keller J. A., Sisquoc L. (eds.), *Boarding school blues. Revisiting American Indian educational experiences*, University of Nebraska Press, Winnipeg 2006.

Trafzer C. E., Keller J. A, Sisquoc L., "Origins and Development of the Indian Boarding School System," in C. E. Trafzer, J. A. Keller, L. Sisquoc (eds.), *Boarding School Blues. Revisiting American Indian Educational Experiences*, University of Nebraska Press, Winnipeg 2006.

Trueba H. T., Delgado-Gaitan C. (eds.), *School & Society: Learning Content Through Culture*, Praeger, New York, Westport and London 1988.

Turner V., "Dewey, Dilthey and Drama: An Essay in the Anthropology of Experience," in V. W. Turner, E. M. Bruner (eds.), *The Anthropology of Experience*, The University of Illinois Press, Urbana and Chicago 1986.

Turner V., *Dramas, Fields, and Metaphors. Symbolic Action in Human Society*, Cornell University Press, Ithaca and London 1974.

Turner V., *On the Edge of the Bush. Anthropology as Experience*, The University of Arizona Press, Tucson 1985.

Tzian L., *Mayas y ladinos en cifras. El caso Guatemala*, Editorial Cholsamaj, Guatemala 1994.

Unger H. G. (ed.), *Encyclopedia of American Education*, Facts on File, New York 2007.
Wax M. L., Diamond S., Gearing F. O. (eds.), *Anthropological Perspectives on Education*, Basic Books, New York and London 1971.
Weber M., *The Protestant ethic and the spirit of capitalism*, Oxford University Press, New York 2001.
Wikan U., *Generous Betrayal. Politics of Culture in the New Europe*, The University of Chicago Press, Chicago and London 2002.
Willet C. (ed.), *Theorizing Multiculturalism: A Guide to the Current Debate*, Blackwell Publishers, Malden and Oxford 1998.

Online resources

http://www.dailymail.co.uk/news/article-2019547/Anjem-Choudary-Islamic-extremists-set-Sharia-law-zones-UK-cities.html [date of entry: 12.12.2013].
http://papers.ssrn. com/sol3/papers.cfm?abstract_id=1303514 [date of entry: 12.12.2013].
http://www.theatlantic.com/magazine/archive/1982/03/broken-windows/304465/ [date of entry: 20.12.13].

Bibliographic note

Some parts of this book were originally published in the following journals and books:

"Interpretation of culture from the perspective of symbolic anthropology," in J. Drozdowicz, *Symbole w działaniu. Akademickie konteksty nurtu symbolicznego w antropologii*, Wyd. Naukowe UAM, Poznań 2009, pp. 218.

"Teaching the *other*. Anthropology of education in the perspective of European cultural dilemmas" [to be published in post-conference proceedings of the 9th Congress of European Culture].

"Culture does matter. The American »boarding schools« system and the transformations of the assimilative policy in the USA," *Studia Edukacyjne*, 17/2011, pp. 201–213.

"Multiculturalism reconsidered. Bilingual education in Guatemala" [to be published in the post-conference proceedings of the conference "Language, Thought and Education: Exploring Networks..."].

"Seeing is believing. Anthropological visions of culture," *Kultura – Społeczeństwo – Edukacja*, 2 (4)/2013 [publishing in progress].

"Domestication of the Orient. Dimensions of the cultural perception of religious otherness in contemporary Europe," *Przegląd Religioznawczy*, 1 (231)/2009, pp. 47–54.

"Between Kwanzaa and Jediism. Contemporary constructions of religious identity and imagined communities," *Przegląd Religioznawczy*, 1 (239)/2011, pp. 179–188.

"Preppers, EDC, and the new millenarianism," *Przegląd Religioznawczy*, 1 (243)/2012 pp. 81–904.

"A pearl in the crown. Concerning Banksy," in A. Cybal-Michalska, P. Wierzba (eds.), *Dyskursy kultury popularnej w społeczeństwie współczesnym*, Wyd. Impuls, Kraków 2012, pp. 49–58.

Ethnologie / Anthropology

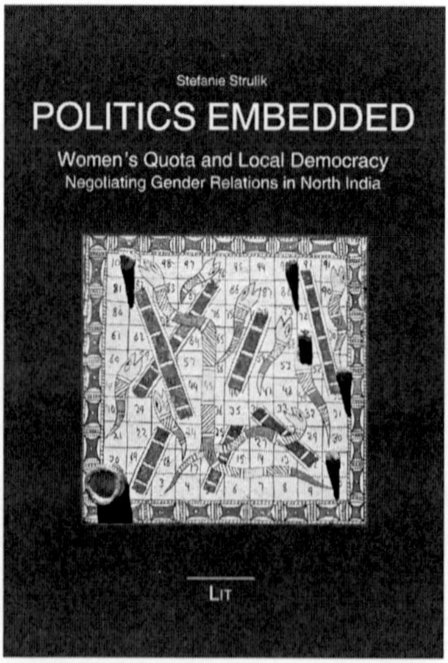

Stefanie Strulik
Politics Embedded
Women's Quota and Local Democracy. Negotiating Gender Relations in North India
A contribution to the anthropology of democracy, this book examines a local governance reform in India – focussing particularly on the 33% women's quota entailed. It highlights the interrelatedness of "doing gender" and "doing politics" and delineates the transformations of gendered political spaces and the shifting boundaries within which women of various castes and classes negotiate the meanings of politics. The book investigates the vernacularization of democracy and analyses local politics as socially embedded – a framework that allows the frictions and contradictions of local politics to be explained without having to take recourse to dichotomies of traditional vs. modern or formal vs. informal politics.
vol. 53, 2014, 400 pp., 50,90 €, br.,
ISBN-CH 978-3-643-80163-0

Susanne Fehlings
Jerewan
Urbanes Chaos und soziale Ordnung
Jerewan ist eine Stadt, die sich auf faszinierende Weise im Bau und Umbau befindet. Mit ihren Gegensätzen aus Ordnung und Unordnung ist sie ein Prisma für viele Entwicklungen und Ereignisse der Vergangenheit, Gegenwart und Zukunft der Region. Dieses Buch beinhaltet eine detaillierte ethnographische Beschreibung des alltäglichen Lebens, der Wohnstrukturen und Bautätigkeiten in der armenischen Hauptstadt. Dabei werden unter anderem soziale Ordnungen sowie sozio-kulturelle Kategorien und Werte im urbanen Raum erfasst.
Bd. 55, 2014, 432 S., 39,90 €, br.,
ISBN 978-3-643-12524-8

LIT Verlag Berlin – Münster – Wien – Zürich – London
Auslieferung Deutschland / Österreich / Schweiz: siehe Impressumsseite